TWICE WOUNDED

John P. F. Lynch

Published by John P F Lynch

Copyright © John P F Lynch 2023

Lynch, John P F
Twice Wounded

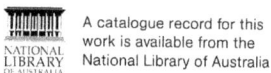
A catalogue record for this work is available from the National Library of Australia

The Author of this book accepts all responsibility for the contents and absolves any other person or persons involved in its production from any responsibility or liability where the contents are concerned.

All rights reserved. No part of this publication may be reproduced, stored in a retrieval system, or transmitted, in any form, by any means, electronic, mechanical, photocopying, recording or otherwise, without prior permission from the author.

Typeset in Bookman Old Style 12 pt

Produced by **TB Books**
P.O. Box 8138
Seymour South Victoria 3660
Email: tbbooks@collings.id.au

Cover Design by TB Books

DEDICATION

To the memory of my uncle Edmund "Boy" Keough of Tocumwal N.S.W.

"Boy" served in the 1st Troop C Sqn. 20th Light Horse Regiment. In December, 1941 they were renamed 20th Motor Regiment and in 1943 they were deployed to New Guinea until April 1945. They were renamed the 20th Pioneer Battalion in April, 1945. The 20th Light Horse Regiment was the only Light Horse Regiment that served overseas during WW2.

CONTENTS

PREFACE vii

INTRODUCTION xi

CHAPTER ONE
    Four Friends.. 13
CHAPTER TWO
    The Recruit... 22
CHAPTER THREE
    Bon Voyage.. 28
CHAPTER FOUR
    The Walers... 35
CHAPTER FIVE
    Overseas Bound... 55
CHAPTER SIX
    The Army Nurse.. 62
CHAPTER SEVEN
    Gallipoli... 73
CHAPTER EIGHT
    England... 87
CHAPTER NINE
    Unusual Assignment.................................. 97
CHAPTER TEN
    France and Belgium.................................. 109
CHAPTER ELEVEN
    Germans Captured 122
CHAPTER TWELVE
    A Dangerous Liaison................................ 125
CHAPTER THIRTEEN
    The Investigation 130
CHAPTER FOURTEEN
    Now the Police 136

CHAPTER FIFTEEN
　Two Meet Again 140
CHAPTER SIXTEEN
　The Sinai 148
CHAPTER SEVENTEEN
　Mary Again 164
CHAPTER EIGHTEEN
　Homeward Bound 169
CHAPTER NINETEEN
　Justice? 177
CHAPTER TWENTY
　Friends No More 182
CHAPTER TWENTY-ONE
　The Hunt 193
CHAPTER TWENTY-TWO
　Pay Back 220
CHAPTER TWENTY-THREE
　Michael's Trial 224
CHAPTER TWENTY-FOUR
　A New Life 240

EPILOGUE 248

DEFINITIONS 251

AUTHOR 254

OTHER BOOKS 256

PREFACE

This most readable historical novel features the realistic adventures experienced by youngsters preparing for active service. From schooldays in country Victoria where most were familiar with horses and outdoor activities, they socialised with boys and girls from similar and different backgrounds at small one-teacher schools, miles from larger communities. They grew up knowing of war because many of their generation had experienced conflict in South Africa, fighting for the British Empire against Dutch settlers during the Boer Wars.

The hero of our novel is eighteen-year-old Jackson Carlsone who, like so many others of his young age, was enticed to join the war effort because of perceived adventure and excitement for new experiences and destinations. The author's understanding of what took place include Jackson's interviews at Melbourne's Victoria Barracks, followed by training at Broadmeadows and subsequent interviews whereby he clearly impressed the officers with his knowledge of the needs and maintenance of horses (specifically Walers). It was explained to him that horses were required for a variety of roles in the military, not just for Light Horse regiments, but also for infantry and artillery. These were times before military armament became mechanised, just twenty years later during the Second World War.

Because of his leadership potential and knowledge of horses, Jackson was offered a commission as Lieutenant into a Light Horse unit. Readers are taken along by the author as Jackson completes the many tasks demanded of him and his men, including the selection and recruitment of hundreds of horses from around country New south Wales.

We then follow Lieutenant Carlsone's experiences on board a troopship as he and thousands of others embarked from Western Australia – destination Cairo – for further acclimatisation training. This inevitably led to the Dardanelles campaign and the risky landings along the shores at Gallipoli – a crusade that was already heading towards disaster. Much of the action described here is verified by Australian journalist, Charles Bean, whose diary of the Gallipoli campaign is amongst the most authentic recollection of what transpired.

Jackson was wounded and spent time recuperating in England. Upon recovery, the newly promoted Captain Carlsone was despatched to the Middle East for service with the Desert Mounted Corps that involved one of the most famous episodes of this campaign. Known as the Charge at Beersheba, this success by the Australian Light Horse allowed the allies access to the valuable water wells necessary for the survival of man and beast. The Turks and their German officers came under attack as the Australians charged the trenches with sharpened bayonets which were replacements for swords that had been left behind at regimental headquarters in Cairo. This was the first of further victories leading to the surrender of all Turkish troops at Damascus. The downfall of the Ottoman Empire that had been in existence since 1300, was the final degradation for the Turkish nation.

At the end of the war, Jackson Carlsone returned home to Victoria, a decorated young man who had achieved the rank of Major, living with experiences far beyond his age and which would remain with him for the rest of his life.

There has been considerable attention to detail wherever available to the author, and there is a basic glossary included to explain some of the early military slang. The use of well-understood and scholarly research enables the reader to 'be there' when much of the action described in this book takes place.

With the author's service background with the Royal Australian Navy, and his passion for recording history from 'the early days', we are sure to see further works from John Lynch on unexplored elements from Australia's past.

Michael Garnett was born in Essex, England in 1938. He attended boarding school in Suffolk, where he was a member of the Combined Cadet Force. Following school, he joined the Royal Air Force for the mandatory National Service commitment, serving on operational deployment to the Far East during the Malaya 'Emergency' of the 1950's.

Mike worked for a London-based company on tea plantations in north-east India (Assam), and later managed an Australian cacao/coconut plantation on the north coast of Papua New Guinea in pre-Independence days. He moved to Australia in 1968 and joined an oil company with which he worked for 26 years. During this time, he joined No. 21 (City of Melbourne) Squadron, Royal Australian Air Force as a reserve officer.

In 2016 he was the recipient of the George Plimpton Award for Sports Journalism instituted by the United States Tennis Association, and in the same year received the Order of Australia Medal (OAM) in the Queen's Birthday Honours List.

He lives in Romsey, Victoria and enjoys visits with his family and six grandchildren.

INTRODUCTION

There are many well-known stories of Australian military engagements in our short history. Some of the most notable are: Eland River in the Boer War; The Charge of the Light Brigade in WW1; The Rats of Tobruk in WW2 and Long Tan during the Vietnam War. These four seem to be the more memorable to the general public. Although this is only an opinion. There are many more depending on your views.

The Australian Light Horse Regiments project an image of the ideal soldier – gallant, swashbuckling and full of bravado. I had an uncle who was a Light Horseman in WW2. He was my idol.

I have been meaning to write a story on the Light Horse but as so much has previously written on their exploits, I decided I would use the Light Horse as a background to this novel. Reading between the lines are some true stories, but generally the story is fiction.

John P F Lynch OAM KSJ FRVAHJ

CHAPTER ONE

Four Friends

The school bell was ringing as Jackson rode his pony into the school paddock. The young schoolboy quickly removed the saddle, blanket and bridle from the pony and carried them to the tack room and hung them on his designated peg. He lived about a mile from the school and, as he had his own pony, he chose to ride to school and not walk.

The Riverbank School was a typical Australian country school, sited in the middle of the town on a four-acre corner block. The Government and Church Organisations had always selected and been granted the choice building blocks. One acre had been fenced to cater for the students who rode their horses to school. The school tack room had been built to store their saddles, blankets and bridles. A horse water trough was alongside the tack room. The students didn't need to feed their horses; the paddock had ample grass all year and the animals would be fed again when the students returned home. Mostly the ponies and horses stood or lay under the shade of the paddock trees.

The headmaster encouraged his students who owned horses, to ride them to school, so long as they were mares, fillies or gelded males. Today the paddock had four ponies and two horses. One of the horses carried two students, who rode their horse without a saddle. It was surprising they didn't fall off!

Jackson reached the classroom doorway as the last student entered. His teacher looked at him but said nothing. Jackson walked to his desk and sat beside his friend, Michael Rawley. The boys' mothers were sisters and the boys had both been born in the same year – 1894.

It was only natural that a close bond formed between them. They fished, hunted, played sport together and then started going to the Saturday night dances with their parents when they became teenagers. A particular incident during their schooldays, bonded their friendship.

Typical of thirteen-year-old boys, they went fishing in the river on a quiet Saturday afternoon. The fish were biting, as they shared sandwiches their mothers had prepared for them. They sat quietly so as not to disturb the fish. They had caught a few and were enjoying their day.

A group of four young horse riders approached them. The riders were senior students at their school; all were known to each other.

The oldest of the riders looked at the fish they had caught and said, 'Those fish are too small. You should throw them back into the river.'

Jackson stood up. 'No, I won't.'

The rider rode up to Jackson and bumped his horse into him, causing him to fall into the river. He was a poor swimmer and began to flounder. Michael instinctively jumped into the river and grabbed Jackson by his shirt collar. Fortunately, the water was only four feet deep and they both were able to reach the bank safely. Jackson was very quiet on the way home. Michael had no idea that Jackson was in a wild fury.

The following Monday at school was to be a day he would never forget. When Jackson saw the rider who bumped him into the water, he walked up to him and punched him in the face. The older boy tried to fight back but Jackson went berserk and the punches from the older boy had no effect on him. Eventually the boy collapsed to the ground and Jackson was about to kick him when the headmaster arrived and grabbed Jackson's coat, pulling him back. Jackson continued struggling but the headmaster was too strong for him.

He picked him up and carried him screaming and kicking to the tack room. After locking the door, he sat down and watched while Jackson slowly settled down.

His years of experience of breaking up schoolyard fights served the headmaster well. He said nothing and waited until Jackson had calmed down enough to look at him.

He asked Jackson, 'Do you want to talk about why you got into the fight?'

Jackson said, 'No.'

'Well, don't do it again, young man. Now off you go to class.'

Michael had told others about what happened at the river and soon the whole town knew of the incident and Jackson's response.

His father was from Calabria in Italy, and it seemed he had inherited his father's fiery nature. The incident was soon forgotten by most, but Michael would remember it in years to come.

Both boys were good students and received credits in most examinations. In Jackson's final year, he was Dux of the school and was offered a scholarship to study for university entry in veterinary medicine.

The offer was a surprise. Jackson worked part time at his uncle's stock horse trading business and, little did he know, that the local veterinarian had noticed how Jackson handled and cared for his uncle's stock horses.

Jackson had always listened intently when he was treating the animals and volunteered to perform minor medical procedures such as injections, cleaning wounds and assisting when a mare was foaling.

Both boys were now seventeen years of age. As Michael was the only son, he was in line to take over his father's saddlery business. They both had promising futures waiting for them.

As teenagers it was inevitable that the two of them would meet girls of a similar age at the local dances, mostly they were from their school. It was at a Saturday dance that the two boys met Jane.

Jane Morris was the daughter of a wealthy farmer. She was a confident sixteen-year-old girl who had spent the last three years at a ladies' convent college in Melbourne. When her mother had a fall from a horse and became a semi-invalid in a wheelchair, Jane had to finish her education early to return home to help her father manage their large property.

She had a good head for figures and soon learned to oversee the farm's finances, guided by the local bank manager.

Jane had a friend, Mary Giles, who was also a farmer's daughter.

The four of them initially met at the Saturday night dances. They soon began to socialise regularly and then to meet midweekly for tea and cake at the town teashop. As the four of them spent more time together, they began to pair off – Jackson with Jane and Michael with Mary. They were a compatible group and thoroughly enjoyed each other's company and interests.

The only difference was – the boys lived in town and the girls lived on their parents' farms. Jackson lived on the outskirts of town with his uncle and aunt on a ten-acre block where his uncle bred and traded stock horses. His parents had moved to Queensland to manage an outback cattle station. Jackson preferred to remain at Riverbank. As a teenager he didn't fancy the loneliness of living in the Australian outback. He had learned to ride at a very early age. His uncle had given him his own pony.

Michael lived with his parents in the middle of town at the back of his father's leather goods shop. He often worked after school and Saturday mornings learning to cut and sew saddles to earn some pocket money.

The girls were interested in breeding a select group of Merino sheep to be shown at local agricultural shows. At times they competed against each other but supported each other, remaining friends. Both girls had won ribbons at previous shows.

Jackson graduated to horse riding in his early teens and when he was old enough, he started to compete in junior rodeos. He was reasonably successful and won a few minor events. He then competed in adult rodeos with limited success. He uncle encouraged him to pursue a career as a veterinarian. He took his advice and accepted the scholarship. It meant he would see less of his friends, but he realised he needed to look to his future and this scholarship could shape his destiny.

Jackson sat with Jane and together they shared their thoughts for their futures. Without realising it, they had grown very close and had deep feelings for each other. They were both now nineteen years of age. The subject of marriage suddenly arose. Jackson hesitatingly asked, 'Would you wait and marry me, until I have completed my studies?'

She immediately answered, 'Yes.' When they told Michael and Mary, they were happy for them.

Saturday night dances were where the community met after their weekly work commitments. Many out-of-towners visited and helped the locals make extended friendships. Alcohol was often a problem for the younger generation. The local constable would show his face during the evening and remain nearby. Over the years, only a few persons had been told to go home.

The four of them were sitting at a corner table, talking, when a young shearer who had had more than a few beers, approached Jane for a dance. Jane declined pleasantly. The young man swore at her and then walked away. Jackson was watching but said nothing. Half an hour later Jane was standing in the hallway waiting for the others. The shearer and a friend approached her. The shearer asked her for a kiss and grabbed her shoulder. As she twisted away her dress tore, and she screamed,

Jackson saw what the shearer had done. He ran to them and pulled the shearer around, punching him hard twice in the face. Stepping back, he hit again and again. The shearer's friend tried to stop Jackson, but he also incurred Jackson's wrath and was savagely punched several times.

The constable soon arrived and eventually stopped the raging Jackson from throwing anymore punches. Both shearers were on the floor semi-conscious and bleeding from facial wounds.

Jane sat on the floor, dazed, watching what was happening. Mary came to her and pulled her torn dress up to cover Jane's bare breast.

The constable arrested the shearer who started the fight. He let his friend go after he had spoken to witnesses.

Those who saw the viciousness of Jackson's fury would not forget it in a hurry. Michael had seen his fury before at school, but not Jane. She was somewhat disturbed by what she had witnessed. Jackson was not a person to cross. He had gone berserk and had been almost uncontrollable and that frightened her. He had a dangerous, mean streak in his genes. She wondered if she really knew him.

Jackson found it difficult being separated from Jane. It was his first time being away from home. He fit in well with his fellow students, but he didn't socialise a great deal. He returned home each fortnight for the weekend by train. The station was only two hundred yards from his uncle's home.

After saying hello to his uncle and aunty, he would saddle up his horse and ride to Jane's property. At times he would stay overnight in her father's shearers' accommodation.

When he approached her father and mother requesting their permission for him to marry their daughter, they agreed. Jane's parents had met Jackson several times before and knew of his studies and his uncle's stock horse business. He impressed them with his confidence and forthright attitude. With his tertiary education and involvement with his uncle's business, they felt he was a suitable person for Jane to marry.

Jackson and Jane agreed that they would become engaged within the next six months and marry within the year. The world was at their feet until an incident happened overseas that would shake this world of theirs with its far-reaching impact.

An assassination of a minor European nobleman caused the start of a world war. With other countries allied to each other in Europe, England joined in the war. Australia, as a member of the British Empire, soon became involved as well, followed by Canada, New Zealand, India and South Africa. Jackson and his friends' destinies were to change.

During a weekend visit to Riverbank, an army recruiting team spent a day in town encouraging young men to join the Australian Imperial Force (AIF). Jackson and Michael listened to the officer extoling the virtue of representing Australia in the fight against an ominous oppressor. Over a beer or two they discussed the recruiting drive. They could see several men sitting at a desk signing enlistment forms. Michael was not interested in leaving home – regardless how good the reason was! Jackson, however, was curious.

He went to the officer and asked to be given an enlistment form and some information sheets. He folded them and put them in his pocket, intending to read them later on the train trip back to Melbourne.

At the university, there was much activity during the week. Several courses were to be ceased. Selected students were to be given accelerated lectures and examinations and, if they were successful, they would be given a Diploma of Veterinary Science, a qualification in lieu of a degree. Jackson found the next two weeks extremely demanding. He had very little sleep during this time, but he was rewarded with a credit pass and a university Diploma Certificate at twenty-one years of age. The presentation day was rushed as was the certificate presentation ceremony. Some university staff were already wearing a uniform. After farewelling his tutors and fellow students Jackson headed for home.

Jane was delighted to have him back in Riverbank. The four of them were together again.

CHAPTER TWO

The Recruit

A month later the recruiting officer and his team were back in town. They placed recruiting banners on several corners, and troopers handed out pamphlets inviting men to join the AIF. Some of the troopers were wearing Boer War medals. Curious potential recruits asked questions such as - What was war like? Naturally the recruiting staff spoke of the adventure of seeing new lands and people. The more gruesome side of war was not mentioned.

When a mother raised an awkward question, she received a short off beat answer from the recruiting officer. War scenarios were not discussed, particularly with mothers in the street.

The war was the topical subject discussed throughout the town. The newspapers were full of war articles. The first contingent of AIF troops had left from Albany in Western Australia on their way to Egypt.

Jackson went to the recruiting table and began to ask the sergeant questions. When he was asked if he was familiar with horses, the officer who was sitting alongside him interrupted. 'I see on your papers that you are a vet.' Jackson nodded. The officer continued, 'What practical experience have you had?'

Jackson told him of the time he spent with his uncle's stock horse business.

The officer took Jackson aside. 'We're looking for veterinarians for the Light Horse Regiments. You're the type of person we need. We're receiving plenty of recruits suitable for the Light Horse Regiments, but we need people who know how to manage the horses at a professional level and who have knowledge over and above an ordinary horseman. If you're interested, could you be at Victoria Barracks Recruiting Office next Wednesday at noon and we could discuss this further?' Jackson nodded in agreement. The officer wrote down his name – Major George Dane – and his office number. He stood up, shook Jackson's hand and went back to his desk.

Jackson stood there wondering – why Victoria Barracks? He was to find it was the main recruiting centre in Melbourne for officers with select skills as well as general recruits.

Before Jackson made up his mind to sign the enlistment paper and be sworn in, he needed to have an in-depth conversation with Jane. Her comments about his intention to join the Australian Light Horse Battalion would decide him – yes or no. He invited Jane to lunch at the hotel to discuss the matter. She nervously wondered what it was all about.

He was waiting outside as she drove up in her two-wheel gig. Jackson tied the horse to a pole and then helped her alight. After a greeting and a quick kiss they entered the restaurant and went to a corner table. He immediately told Jane that he was thinking of joining the army.

She sat quietly absorbing his words, thinking of the implications this could have on their future. Her father had served in the Boer War and had told her of some of his escapades. Some good! Some bad! He had only been away for twelve months and had returned unscathed.

She told Jackson of her father's Boer War experience and his time away from home. With the number of local young men who were enlisting, she could understand his dilemma. They both agreed to think it over for a week and meet for lunch the next week. Jackson changed the subject to local gossip, although the war was mostly the only topic on everyone's mind.

The following week Jackson travelled to Victoria Barracks to meet with Major Dane. At the barracks he was surprised to see a line of men stretching for several hundred yards going to a building with a large sign "Recruitment Centre". He continued to the main gate and an army guard pointed out the way to Major Dane's office. He arrived five minutes before noon and knocked on the office door. It was opened by Major Dane, who invited him into his office.

His office had been laid out as an interview room, with a table and three chairs on one side and a single chair opposite them. He was introduced to the other two officers and directed to sit. He recognised one of the other officers as a veterinary medicine lecturer from his university days.

Major Dane chaired the interview. After introducing the other officers, who were captains, he asked Jackson to relate his experienced with stock horses.

Jackson spoke of his uncle's horse breeding business and what tasks he had been carrying out over the last two years. At one stage the lecturer asked a technical question regarding the treatment of specific injuries to horses' hocks.

Jackson answered the question correctly. After two more technical questions, which he answered satisfactorily, Major Dane asked him, 'What do you know of the Waler breed of horses?'

Jackson told him they had bred some of them and they were excellent stock horses. They were intelligent, had a good temperament, were alert, had straight strong legs, strong rounded backs and deep hind quarters. Stockmen and drovers preferred them over any other breed.

The major asked, 'Do you have any particular interests or hobbies?'

'When I had time, I competed in rodeos.'

The major stood up. 'Well, we will exempt you from the riding test.' He nodded slightly to the other officers. 'Jackson, could you please wait outside?'

Ten minutes later he was invited back into the interview room. The table had been pushed to one side and the chairs were in a circle. The major spoke first. 'As I previously mentioned, the AIF Light Horse Regiments are seeking competent veterinary staff. With your experience and qualifications, we are offering you a commission as a lieutenant. You would be attached to the Australian Light Horse. If you accept, you will be required to report here within fourteen days. Would you like to give it some thought before you make up your mind?'

Jackson was quietly delighted and paused before he answered. 'I need to talk with my fiancée, but yes, I am interested in joining the Light Horse.'

They accepted his answer, which was a normal response, and he agreed to report to Major Dane in seven days.

Jackson used the evening train trip home to think of the pros and cons of going to war or not going to war. Working for a stock breeder, he knew he would probably be exempt from military service. But he felt he had an obligation to enlist, like most of the other local men of his age. His uncle, and others, said the war would be over within the year. He was sure his relationship with Jane would survive a year apart.

Jane was waiting at the station platform when he arrived home. They kissed each other and walked to Jackson's uncle's home to have dinner. His dogs were loose, and they had the house to themselves. Normally the dogs would be chained at their kennels if his uncle was home. Together they cooked a quick and easy meal.

After dinner they sat on the porch. The breeze from the river was welcome after the heat of the day. Jane started. 'Well?'

Jackson looked at her in the moonlight. Nodding to her he told her he had been accepted as a veterinary officer with the Australian Light Horse, if he wished to enlist. 'I would like to enlist but only if you're happy for me to do so.'

Jane had been thinking of this moment for the last few days and she had the same answer for yes or no. She put her arms around him and said, very wisely, 'The final decision is yours and I will abide by it. What is twelve months when we have agreed to spend the rest of our lives together? I think it is very brave of you to volunteer to fight for your country. Also, I realise if you don't go you will always wonder whether you should have gone to the war or not.'

Jackson was quite surprised at Jane's logic. She was right. He would enlist.

The news was soon around town, and wherever he went he was greeted with a friendly wave or a handshake and a 'Well done.' Particularly from the Boer War veterans.

CHAPTER THREE

Bon Voyage

There were four other volunteers departing with Jackson. Before they departed, the town council decided to put a on a dinner at the local hotel to farewell the five volunteers. The hotel had a large outdoor covered-in area, which could seat around a hundred people.

A notice was placed on the post office door asking for the names of people who would be attending the seven p.m. dinner. The final count was ninety persons. The town's dance band started playing at six forty-five and they played until ten p.m., giving their services for free, albeit for a free beer or two.

The meals were prepared by a local women's gardening group and naturally was a basic country fare – corn soup, roast lamb and vegetables followed by sponge roll and custard. After the tables were cleared, the speeches began. Although there were several speakers, they wisely kept their presentations to a minimum.

The last speaker had been a lieutenant in the Boer War and gave a quick description of his travels and the sights he had enjoyed. His final deed was to call each of the five volunteers forward.

On behalf of the shire council and the local citizens, he presented each of them with a tribute medal to acknowledge their commitment to Australia and the British Empire. The medal was bronze with the local shire's seal on the obverse and the soldier's name on the reverse side. The medal was in an attractive black box, together with a green and wattle gold ribbon. He then wished them 'Bon Voyage' and three cheers.

Each soldier was invited to speak but only Jackson took up the offer. He had come prepared and had written a short dialogue. He thanked the councillors and the local citizens. He then spoke of family support while they were away. 'Please don't forget us. Keep writing letters and pray for our safe return. Hopefully we will all be home by Christmas.' The entire room stood up, cheering and clapping. It was a memorable evening.

It was time for them to leave and become soldiers. Half of the Riverbank's citizens were at the station to farewell Jackson and the other four recruits. They each made quick goodbyes. As expected, the women cried, and the men looked serious. The towns' people kept waving until the train disappeared out of sight.

On its way to Melbourne the train stopped several times, and the railway station scene was repeated. Each station had recruits who were farewelled with kisses and handshakes and, of course, the expected tears. Sandwiches were shared as was the water or tea. The young recruits were excited and viewed the war as an adventure.

The four other locals were heading to the army recruit camp at Broadmeadows. A small town around twenty miles north of Melbourne.

Jackson shook hands with the Riverbank recruits before they left the train at Broadmeadows, wishing them good luck. He had read that when Australia joined in the war, the Broadmeadows camp had been established within a matter of weeks. The Defence Department had moved into top gear. The camp was laid out, water piped in, telephones were connected, hundreds of tents neatly laid out, picket lines for horses installed, even a postal service arranged.

Three thousand recruits arrived within the first two weeks of war being declared. The four recruits from Riverbank were now just service numbers, along with three thousand other new recruits. In a way, Jackson was disappointed that he would not see it.

The camp recruits could be posted to a number of different areas – the Light Horse, artillery, machine gunnery, infantry, signals or the many other support groups, depending on what qualifications they had. If they had no specific qualification, they were probably destined for the infantry as a "foot slogger".

Jackson continued to Flinders Street Station, Melbourne's main railway station and then he walked to Victoria Barracks, a distance of about a mile.

After meeting Major Dane and completing the administration requirements, he was taken to the Supply Department and fitted out with his uniform and the other equipment he would need.

The uniform consisted of a khaki jacket, breeches, braces, riding boots, a Sam Brown belt, shoulder strap and holster, fur felt hat with chin strap. A water bottle and haversack were included plus underclothes and toiletries.

Later he would acquire further equipment as a vet officer. Troopers were issued with a uniform, a bandoleer, a revolver and a rifle and bayonet plus haversack, blanket and other necessities.

The next day, Jackson was directed to a training school for an indoctrination class, together with other new officers. As an officer, it was expected he would have confidence and presentation skills. Each officer had a choice of subjects, relating to his appointment. For his subject, Jackson spoke of the origin of the Waler breed and his personal knowledge of its attributes including the best way to handle and care for this breed of horse. The training officer was so impressed by his unique knowledge, he asked him to do a second presentation to over a hundred Light Horsemen. Jackson used a megaphone to ensure he could be heard.

He spent several weeks at the training school attending lectures covering military protocols, history of the British Army, marching drills, handling firearms including a visit to the rifle range and, not to forget, the army bible, "The Rules Manual". The army had manuals for everything. Then finally, he attended a Passing Out Parade. He was now a commissioned Australian army officer.

After the morning parade, Jackson received his orders, advising him that he was entitled to a seven-day leave pass prior to reporting for duty as required in his orders. He returned to his room to pack his clothes and manuals.

Dressed in his Light Horse uniform complete with the emu feather and Sam Brown belt and empty revolver holster, he looked in the mirror and allowed himself a nod of satisfaction. Now with a full set beard he looked every inch an Australian Light Horse officer.

He had written to Jane as soon as he knew of his leave entitlement. When he arrived in Riverbank early in the evening she was waiting with Michael. When they both saw him in his uniform, they clapped and bowed to him. Jackson laughed, kissed Jane and then shook Michael's extended hand.

Jane had booked a table for two at the hotel. Michael had prudently declined to dine with them as they had only a few days together and no doubt would not want to share their time.

They sat opposite each other. Jane began telling him of the town gossip and Jackson nodded politely, but really, he was just admiring her, well dressed and very attractive. He was so happy that she loved him; he barely heard a word she said.

Finally, she said, 'You've not heard a word I've said. *You* can talk now. It's your turn. Tell me about your army life and I *will* listen.'

He laughed and nodded. He told her about the training school. His tuition had covered everything from military drills, brigade structures, protocols, decorum, mess rules and, most importantly, leadership and responsibility to his men.

As a veterinary officer he was exempt from the normal training of line officers, such as drills in tactics, armoury, etc. Although, he had been taken to the pistol range and taught how to use a revolver, he would only carry one when on duty.

The two of them met each afternoon and spent a few hours talking about their future upon his return from overseas. Sometimes they went riding. Other times they walked along the river path to their favourite spot.

It was a shady nook, surrounded on three sides by large bushes and with ample grass. They lay on the grass listening to the water's rippling sound as it flowed over the large rocks and watched the water flowing by. It was the ultimate peaceful haven on earth, as far as the two of them were concerned.

The day before he was to return to Melbourne, they took a small picnic lunch with them. They were both pensive. They expected to be apart for twelve months. Jackson kissed her passionately and she returned his ardour. Slowly he unbuttoned her dress and put his hand on her naked breast.

It was the first time the two of them had shown their deep yearnings. Jane was unsure how far they should go.

She was a virgin and she had promised her mother she would try to keep her virginity until her wedding night.

She sat upright and looked down at Jackson, who had an inquiring look on his face. Her honest statement did not really surprise him. However, he told her he understood and respected her wish. They would both wait until that night.

Jane said, 'You unbuttoned my dress, so you can button it up'. Before he did so he pulled her down and kissed her breast and gave it a little squeeze. She enjoyed the moment. He helped her to her feet, repacked the picnic hamper, and they walked arm in arm back to town.

Several of the townsfolk knew Jackson was departing to the unknown and were at the station to farewell him.

After shaking hands and receiving a few kisses, he turned to Michael and said, 'I want you to look after Jane. I want your word of honour.'

Michael said, 'Trust me, I will.'

Jackson shook his hand and turned to Jane. They had said their goodbyes yesterday. They kissed tenderly. He turned quickly and boarded the train, a tear in his eye. Jane was quietly crying, standing alongside Michael. They waved to each other until the train disappeared in the distance.

CHAPTER FOUR

The Walers

Lieutenant Jackson Carlsone reported to the Australian Light Horse Training Camp and presented his papers to the duty officer. The officer welcomed him and then escorted him to the office of the Commanding Officer Colonel Stanley Owens DSC. He was the senior veterinary officer and a veteran of the Boer war.

The colonel welcomed him. 'Your arrival is timely. It's good to see you. We need a man with your veterinary qualifications and horse breeding experience. We are presently into a large project of buying horses.

'Your first assignment will be to go to New South Wales next week and buy as many horses as you can. You will have an experienced sergeant and corporal and ten troopers as your squad.

'They will show you the military way we do things. As you no doubt know, we also need horses for some infantry battalions, towing artillery, ambulance wagons, etc. However, I would prefer you to only buy Walers. You will be briefed further over the next few days. My aide will show you your quarters. Dismissed.' Jackson saluted and left the colonel's office.

The aide took him to a large wooden building. It had sleeping quarters, a small room with a bed, a small desk and a single chair. A clothes rack was in one corner and a small chest of drawers. It was clean and looked comfortable. There was a tack room for officers' saddles and riding gear at the rear of the building.

Although Jackson tried to hide his disappointment at not being posted to an operational Light Horse Brigade, he accepted his allotted task and began to look forward to the coming weeks.

After the parade the next morning, the colonel, realising his disappointment, approached him and advised him, 'You will be posted to an operation brigade when you return.'

Jackson then met with his squad. They looked to be very fit and capable Horsemen and he noted they were all older than him. After they were introduced, he spoke with each soldier and asked them their marriage status and where they were from. His interest impressed them, as some officers had not even learnt their names. He was more mature than they thought.

The next few days were an eye opener. Jackson was glad he had two experienced NCOs in his team. They knew the army system and how to get around restrictions. Jackson had the vet expertise, and they had the army experience. One of his first tasks was to select a horse for himself and then collect his riding gear and saddle bags. The sergeant had a good eye for a good reliable horse and had already corralled six horses for him to select. He selected a four-year-old gelding. It was sturdy, deep chested with powerful withers. The sergeant nodded his approval; his officer knew horses. Jackson walked the horse around the corral looking at the way he moved.

The horse had been broken in but had not been ridden for a month. Jackson spoke quietly to the horse while he patted his neck. Slowly he placed the saddle blanket on his back. The horse remained calm. When he felt the weight of the saddle, he became a little difficult when the billets were being tightened to the girth belt. Eventually the saddle was in place and secured.

Jackson continued to walk him and then, suddenly, he swung himself up into the saddle. The horse shied and bucked a few times, then gave a few small jumps before trotting. His squad had been watching, to judge their officer's horsemanship, and they agreed he knew horses. He didn't tell them he was a rodeo rider. Regardless of his youth, he was now totally accepted by them as a fellow Australian Light Horseman and their leader

The briefing was carried out by the colonel. Each lieutenant was handed a small leather satchel. Inside were their detailed orders. Five squads of Light Horseman were in attendance. Jackson's squad was assigned the northwest area of New South Wales. The others were going to Queensland and southwest area of New South Wales.

The Walers had been in demand since the late 1800s in India. They were now in demand in England and for the Australian Light Horse Regiments overseas.

Jackson read his briefing papers. They stated the Walers must be – between five and twelve years of age, short back, good shoulders, deep girth, fifteen hands high and carry sixteen stone (rider plus gear). Jackson could have added a few more preferences, which he would have included in his selection criteria, in particular the animal's gait and the condition of the animal's hoofs.

A suggested price of thirty pounds was included. The Walers were believed to have been bred from brumbies and thoroughbreds and were said to have originated in New South Wales, hence their name "Walers". They were popular with stockmen.

At the end of the briefing, the colonel drew him aside. He remembered seeing the disappointed look on Jackson's face previously. He had seen it many times before.

He told Jackson, 'Be assured, as I said, you will be posted overseas at the completion of your horse purchasing assignment.' The colonel turned and walked away, not waiting for a response. Jackson stood there both surprised and delighted with the good news. He wrote to Jane that night telling her of his most eventful week.

The rest of the departure week was spent arranging their schedule and identifying any supplies they would not be able to purchase en route. Jackson had a medical kit and one of the troopers had been a former blacksmith and had a portable shoeing kit. Two dozen horseshoes were included plus two spare saddles and bridles. They decided to take three spare horses. They would carry their spares and be a backup if a squad member's horse became incapacitated for any reason. Food, water containers, some horse fodder plus water bags and camping gear completed their supplies.

Lieutenant Carlsone carried a letter of authority from the Australian Army Finance Department to purchase goods relevant to his written orders.

Each of the riders had their saddles bags and haversack filled with a change of clothing, a few personal odds and ends and various items for tending to their horse such as a curry comb and hoof care products. A bedroll was tied to the rear of their saddle or cantle. Jackson had a revolver; the others carried a carbine in their saddle holsters and a bayonet on their waist belt. A double-sided cartridge belt was slung over each trooper's left shoulder. Their guns were mainly for show, but they would be used by them; they were soldiers and would react as necessary if they had interference with their military duties, such as watching over the purchased army horses.

On the day of departure, the five squads were assembled at the morning parade. They performed a march past, with the colonel taking the salute. Each lieutenant led his squad, followed by the sergeant, and two rows of five troopers. The second row of troopers were leading the three spare horses with their supplies.

A corporal brought up the rear. It was a small unimportant parade, but not to Jackson. He felt very proud and wished Jane were there to see him. The sun was shining with flags fluttering in the morning breeze. How good could it get? He was in his element.

They rode their horses to the local railway station, arriving an hour before it was due to depart for Sydney. The horses were loaded into the rear freight van stalls. Two troopers at a time stayed in the freight van with the horses, changing over at each stop. Jackson stayed with the rest of his squad in the passenger carriage next to the van.

When the train stopped for an hour to take on water and coal, the horses were fed and watered, then walked for ten minutes and reloaded. The train trip took seven hours, and it was getting dark by the time the horses were unloaded.

The local army barracks was nearby, and the sergeant went ahead to advise their expected arrival.

The duty officer nodded to him. 'Yes, you were expected.' He pointed out the stables and the sleeping quarters. There were signs advising who went where. If they were there within an hour of the canteen closure, a hot meal would be available. The squad arrived ten minutes later and, after stabling the horses and a quick wash, the men went to the hall for their meal.

After seeing the horses settled, Jackson went with the duty officer to the mess, where a cook immediately appeared with a hot meal. After dining, a steward escorted him to the visitors' quarters and the men to a dormitory. He then sat down and wrote up his diary and then a letter to Jane. He had enjoyed his first day as an officer in command of his small squad. He finished the day with a shower and soon fell into a deep sleep.

The bugle call was unwelcomed but was a fact of military life and had been so for countless years.

He dressed quickly and went to the officers' mess hoping to be one of the first there. He was impatient to get moving on their next train journey, heading out west.

After breakfast he walked to the horse stalls and found his squad were all up and about, busy watering and feeding their horses. They had all inspected their hoofs and shoes. Jackson did the same as his men. He was pleased with his squad. Over the days he had got to know each of them on a personal basis – family, home, etc. The sergeant assembled the squad at the guard house and waited for the protocols to be carried out.

Lieutenant Carlsone thanked the officer of the day for his barrack's hospitality. He mounted his horse and saluted and lead the squad out onto the road to the railway siding.

Jackson's orders were to proceed to Bathurst by rail and then by road to Sterling Station, Allen Station and, finally, Walla Station. A map of the district was enclosed. However, the map lacked detail. Particularly, water courses. As the squad was to find out later. Each of the three cattle stations had approximately one hundred brumbies for sale. The horses had been placed in the home paddocks close to the homesteads, ready for collection so were no longer running wild.

By the time Jackson was due to arrive it was required that all horses would be 'saddle broken' and ready to ride. Although a rider would need to treat the horse as semi-wild until he bonded with his selected horse.

The squad's destination was to the west-northwest area of New South Wales where the country was hot, dry and arid. It was surprising that the brumbies survived in such an inclement environment, but they did. They were very tough horses. One could understand why the stockmen and drovers preferred them.

The railway siding manager had expected them and advised their train would depart early afternoon. After tending to the horses, the squad had a meal in a local hotel with a beer or two as they discussed their orders.

Jackson asked if any of them had been out west before. Two troopers had worked in the far west several years ago. The outback country's biggest problem was water.

'We must be aware where we are able to get water for the horses,' one said. Upon being asked to describe the area and what problems they may have droving up to one hundred horses to a distant railway siding, the other trooper said, 'If the horses have been "broken in" and gelded, we should be able to control them.'

The first trooper nodded in agreement. 'Sometimes a rogue horse emerges. Watch him and we'll be all right.'

Jackson asked the sergeant if he wished to comment.

'No,' he agreed. 'As long as we don't have a disruptive horse, we should be okay. If we have one, he must be shot immediately. Droving one hundred horses can be done. They have a herd mentality, but we must remain alert all the time.' He added, 'We must ensure water is available en route. We need good local maps.'

Jackson nodded. 'I asked the colonel before we left to contact the stations and have accurate water maps available for us on arrival.'

Their horses were loaded onto open cattle carriages and separated by portable dividers. The two troopers scrounged some straw bales and were comfortably lounging in their "ad lib" couches. Jackson and the remainder of his squad were seated in a carriage in front of the horse carriage as before. The train left on time, travelling west up and through the Great Dividing Mountain Range and then into a completely new environment. The range separated the green coastal plains from the dry inland plains. The picturesque towering mountains, together with the magnificent trees hundreds of years old was a sight he would not forget. There were colourful birds, an occasional wallaby and a few log cabins with smoke rising slowly into the sky from their chimneys. A few people waved.

The sun was setting and casting long shadows down in the valleys. He must describe the sight of this scenery to Jane – if he could find the right words. The train stopped four times for passengers and freight. Two of the longer stops were for water.

The troopers in the horse carriage were relieved at each stop but the horses were not exercised. Jackson felt they had had enough exercise walking from the barracks.

They arrived at their destination an hour after sunrise. It was a typical Australian country town, notably – several pubs, wide streets, horse drawn carts and dogs. After feeding and watering the horses they had breakfast at a small café. The owner was a Boer War veteran and recognised the sergeant's medal ribbons. After inviting him to sit with them, they exchanged pleasantries.

Jackson told him they were on their way to Sterling Station to purchase horses. He asked, 'Is there a preferred track for droving a hundred horses from Sterling Station back to this siding?'

The veteran answered, 'Yes! Cattle men have been using it for years. I'll draw you a map. It will save you time and worry. It will take you around eight days droving.' The map he drew was neat and with several noticeable landmarks such as a small hill, two creeks and an unusual large rock.

He also had a north arrow on the map. The track appeared to be fairly straight and had been an old river course. He advised, 'As you leave town, take the left fork and head to the large rock outcrops, then follow the map. You'll find the station easily.'

After thanking the café owner, the squad headed to the local Agriculture Show Ground to camp the night. They would head to Sterling Station the next morning.

One of the troopers was an accomplished cook and took charge of the meals. He was adamant he wanted no help; they all offered but were pleased when he refused. Although the sergeant did buy rump steaks in town for him.

The meal was appreciated; he was a good cook. Jackson's troopers each seemed to have a particular skill.

Next morning, they carried out their usual routines. Bedrolls, saddlebags and equipment were all resecured onto the spare horses. As they rode through town, pedestrians waved and wished them luck.

The sergeant thought, *they may be thinking, we're off to the war.*

They soon found the fork in the road and turned left. They rode all day, except for two meal breaks. As the sun was going down, it was decided to camp overnight. There were no steaks this time.

It was enjoyable sleeping under the stars. That a war should be raging somewhere in the world seemed almost unbelievable, when here in the Australian country outback, there was such tranquillity. The silence was peaceful and looking at the stars so relaxing. Except for the horses, the only sound was a dingo howling way off in the distance

The next morning became one of concern. As he was dressing, one of the troopers was bitten on his calf muscle by a snake. The snake had vanished, but the trooper's yell got everybody's attention.

Jackson immediately cut open his trouser leg. Two small bite marks were obvious. Jackson used a scalpel and cut through the holes. While he was doing this the corporal tied a tourniquet to his upper leg. Jackson placed a suction pump over the bleeding cut and tried to extract the venom still in the bite area. The trooper was sweating and very drowsy. There was very little else they could do.

He hadn't seen the snake. Jackson looked at the trouser leg where he had been bitten and was heartened to see the entry marks were in a very thick part of the trouser materiel. On the inside of the materiel was a large area of moisture – it was almost certain to be venom. The trooper may not have much venom injected into his leg. They could only watch and wait. The squad troopers took turns watching him during the night.

The next morning, they were delighted to see the trooper wide awake and smiling. He only had a headache, but Jackson decided he should remain and rest and follow them in a day or so. A trooper stayed with him.

The squad continued to follow the old water course which had several waterholes. After six days they were looking down on Sterling Downs. It was alongside a wide creek. There were several large sheds, living quarters for the stockmen, some smaller buildings, and two homesteads. Several large holding paddocks were adjacent the sheds. One paddock had a very large mob of horses. They rode into the station and were greeted by several barking cattle dogs, not dangerous, just friendly. A tall and impressive man waved to them from the veranda of the larger homestead. He welcomed them. He was the owner, James Edwards, and invited them into a large covered-in veranda. A servant was requested to serve tea and scones, a typical visitors' repast. The scones were accompanied with cream and strawberry jam – a rare delicacy for soldiers.

James Edwards was the son of a pioneer of these parts. During tea, he told them that over the years his family had endured droughts and floods, but they were a hardy family and had survived.

In the early days the Aborigines had clashed with them but now ten of his stockmen were local Aborigines. James advised Jackson his troopers could sleep in the large bunkhouse for his station hands. After bringing in the brumbies, the hands had been given a week off and most went to the nearest town. Jackson and the NCOs were offered his brother's homestead. It was fully furnished; his brother now lived in Sydney.

After tea, Jackson dismissed the corporal and the troopers. The sergeant and he sat down to talk business.

James started and advised he had two hundred brumbies. He owned a hundred and the other hundred were from Allen Station.

The owner of Allen Station had a contract to deliver twenty brumbies to a horse broker. As he was coming close by Sterling Station, he had decided to bring his hundred Walers there. Being away from the station, he was worried he might miss the military buyer.

This suited Jackson. It would save weeks of travel. 'We'll have to inspect each horse,' said Jackson.

James nodded agreement and advised that all horses had been 'broken in'.

Late that afternoon, the other two troopers arrived. The snake bite victim had fully recovered.

The following morning, the inspections began. James had installed a very narrow wooden chute between two paddocks. The chute would only allow one horse at a time to enter. It was usually used to load a valuable bull or stallion onto an enclosed wagon to service cows or mares on neighbouring stations. The chute was laid flat on the ground. When a horse entered, both exits were closed. The horse then had a noose placed around its neck and pulled tight by a trooper.

Jackson then looked closely at the horse's condition, muscle tone etc. As the horses had been running wild, he did not expect their coat to shine. A curry comb would soon have their coats shiny. Their hoofs were unshod. He looked to see if any were cracked. When the horse was released both the sergeant and he watched the horse closely to see if it moved smoothly or if it favoured a leg when trotting or walking.

The inspection of two hundred horses took over four days. Several horses were reinspected due to their gait. Two were rejected due to age and two due to awkward movement when trotting. Overall, Jackson was impressed with the quality of the mob. The horses were sturdy, alert and would definitely be an asset to the Light Horse Regiments.

Jackson was aware of the prices of horses and successfully negotiated a figure agreeable to both parties.

The squad had a meeting to work out the best way to take the mob to the railway siding. They decided to do two trips of a hundred horses at a time. They would follow the same track they had travelled to Sterling Downs.

Over the next month they successfully completed their tasks. The experience of the squad kept the mobs together. Twice they had a few runaways, but they were soon caught and headed back to their mob.

They all gave a sigh of relief when the first mob was finally driven into the railway sidings paddocks. Freight trains departed three times a week. After the first mob were loaded, the squad returned to Sterling Downs and repeated the droving. When the last of the horses were loaded at the siding, they had two days rest in town. They had earned it.

Now they headed to Walla Station. Their map showed Walla Station was further out west than Sterling Downs. The map was not very detailed in description.

It only showed a few landmarks, such as water courses, significant hills or watering holes. It gave no indication whether the water holes were dry or not. After a few days, Jackson sent out two troopers to head forty-five degrees left of their track and two more troopers forty-five degrees right of their track. They were to return the next day. The rest would continue to follow the map.

The weather was dry, hot and dusty and they had to endure small eddies of dust several times daily. The worst of the dust was the effect it had on their eyes. It made them dry, itchy, stinging and painful. They discovered a wet cloth helped a little to wipe and wash their eyes.

Water was of concern until, surprisingly, a small clump of trees revealed a large freshwater pool. Jackson marked this on the map. After bathing their eyes, the men enjoyed a real bath in the cool waters, not just an ABC wash. The horses were watered, and every container was filled with water. They decided to camp there that evening.

As they were breaking camp next morning, the two troopers who had headed left returned with good news. They had met some drovers who gave directions to Walla Station. It was only two days' ride. Jackson left one of these two troopers to wait for the other two and show them the way to join the squad.

Walla Station was in a valley – a large homestead surrounded by several large buildings. The area looked barren and arid. There was a dry creek bed with some water pools, half a mile from the homestead. Each building had a water tank and roof gutters. Horses could be seen milling around in a home paddock.

There were several people waiting for them to arrive. They had seen their dust in the distance. A middle-aged man with a large hat stepped forward. He was Edgar James, the manager, who welcomed them. He commented they had been expected to arrive within the week.

The squad was taken to a large shed which was a dining room for the station hands. The manager introduced his two foremen and Jackson reciprocated. Over tea and cake, they engaged in small talk.

After their accommodation had been organised, Edgar James, his two foremen, Jackson and his NCO's sat down to talk business. Edgar advised that he had followed the requirements in the military purchase agreement. 'We have one hundred and fifty horses in the paddock. They have all been broken in and are in good condition.'

Both of his foremen nodded in agreement.

Jackson replied, 'Thank you. I am required to inspect each horse.'

Edgar answered, 'If you wish I could bring in a vet.'

Jackson told him he was a vet. and he would like to start the inspection tomorrow morning.

Walla Station did not have a chute. Each horse had to be lassoed to be inspected. With the help of the station hands, who were most capable, this time-consuming inspection was successfully completed within three days. Only two horses were rejected; both were under thirteen hands high.

However, an ugly incident occurred when a foreman started whipping a horse that refused to stand still. Jackson watched him for a while and then approached him. 'Stop!' he yelled.

'I know what I'm doing,' the foreman said. He then hit the horse on the face.

Jackson grabbed the whip from him. 'No more. Enough is enough.'

The foreman turned around and punched Jackson on the jaw, knocking him down.

Jackson sat there for a few seconds and then stood up. He walked to the foreman and started swinging punches. The foreman hit Jackson a few times, but Jackson didn't seem to feel them. Jackson continued throwing punches at the dazed foreman who was holding onto the fence. Jackson did not stop throwing punches until the sergeant and the corporal pulled him away.

Slowly Jackson calmed down.

The foreman slid to the ground and rolled over onto his side. He was bleeding profusely from his nose and mouth. Several teeth were missing and both eyes were almost closed.

Jackson's squad and some station hands who saw the brutal thrashing he gave the foreman were amazed at Jackson's ferocity. They now knew he was not a man to be trifled with.

The following morning Jackson and Edgar agreed on the purchase price for the horses.

Edgar had some station hands going to the railway siding to collect supplies for Walla Station. He offered them to him to help with droving the mob.

Jackson gratefully accepted the offer. Before he departed, he apologised to the foreman for losing his temper. They shock hands but the foreman didn't seem very happy.

They opened the paddock gate, and the drovers moved the mob slowly towards the opening. The mob was a little difficult at first, but they soon grouped together and moved quietly.

One horse was of concern. He was a big gelding and continually tried to bite the other horses. This caused them to get agitated and try to break away from the mob.

Jackson and the sergeant watched this occur for about half an hour.

The sergeant shook his head. 'He's going to be a problem.'

Jackson said, 'I'll fix it.' He rode over to the horse and drew his revolver. He shot the horse between the eyes. They left the carcase where it fell. They all knew it would soon become a meal for eagles, dingos and all the other outback scavengers. Only his bones would remain.

The mob was easy to handle and remained reasonably well packed. There were a few stragglers, but they were soon rounded up and returned to the mob. The night stops kept the drovers' alert. The dingo howls were annoying, but the horses remained reasonably calm.

One could see the Walers were intelligent animals. They had a particular look about them that other horses didn't have. They stood proudly, their heads erect, and ears pointed upright.

They had an easy and leisurely return trip this time. The stockmen were most capable and kept the mob tight with little trouble. They knew where water was available and, happily, there were no dust storms. The droving was successfully completed and saved a few days. All the horses were in good condition.

After thanking the station drovers, Jackson went to the rail siding manager's office and was delighted to find he had mail from Jane. He was also advised cattle carriages were available for immediate loading of the entire mob. The train would be leaving early the next morning. It took several hours to water and feed the horses and then load them. The team then set up camp at the local Agriculture Show Ground and went off to the pub for a meal and a few well-earned ales.

Jackson had forgotten just how many weeks they had been away. They had first departed this railway siding two months ago and were all naturally delighted to have mail waiting for them. Lieutenant Jackson Carlsone also received a telegram from Colonel Owens.

He would read it after he read Jane's letters. Jane had written six letters and had dated them on the outside of the envelope. He found a quiet corner and sat down, eagerly opening and then reading her letters. She was happy receiving his letters and had expected delays in answers to hers, realising he was away from towns – in the outback! The local gossip made him feel comfortable and not so far away. He recognised most of the names she wrote about and he could imagine the scenarios she described or mentioned.

As always Michael and Mary sent their kind wishes for his safe return. He sat quietly absorbing Jane's loving words.

Jackson then opened the army telegram. They were his orders for his posting as promised by Colonel Owens. On receipt of these orders, he and his squad were to proceed immediately to the Sydney docks and report to Colonel Wayne Spry, the Australian Light Horse Liaison Officer for further orders. He was also to advise the final count of Walers delivered to the railway siding, which he did immediately. The colonel promptly responded with a, 'Well done – three hundred and forty-five Walers – excellent.'

When he told his squad their orders, they also were disappointed, but they were in the army and there was a war on. No leave! So be it!

The train left on time with the squad and the Walers. The return journey was spent catching up on their sleep. Their mounts needed a break as well as the squad; they would soon have their shiny coats again. The extra time available was spent giving their mounts a good curry combing.

Colonel Spry asked Jackson to be seated. He thanked him for his excellent mob of horses. His vets had not rejected one horse. This was the first time this had happened. He asked, 'What is the average age of the horses?'

Jackson answered, 'Seven years.'

The colonel replied, 'I've ear-marked these horses for a Light Horse Regiment. If I had my way, you would be sent outback again. Your skilful selection is out of the ordinary.'

Jackson accepted this as a compliment. 'I'd rather be in a Light Horse Regiment, sir.'

The colonel nodded. 'I can understand, and you have your wish. You and your squad are being posted to Egypt on the next ship available.' The colonel paused. 'Which is in three days. Coincidently, your Walers are going on the same ship. You will be required to assist the dockers in loading them safely. All up, there will be six hundred horses on board. Food stocks have already been loaded.

'Army personnel heading for Gallipoli will assist your troopers in tending the horses. You are one of three vets on board and you each will be answerable to the Light Horse Regimental Commander, Colonel Hewlett.'

He continued, 'Your squad's task is to care for the mounts en route to Cairo. Upon arrival, you will proceed to the main remount station. You are expected, and you will receive further orders on arrival. It has been suggested that you may be going to Gallipoli, but it is not confirmed as yet. With few experienced vets available, the regiments' demands change constantly, not only for the Light Horse but for the artillery gun carriages, ambulances etc. However, I would like to think the Walers are only for the Light Horse Regiments.

'Thank you, Lieutenant Carlsone. My aide will show you where to go. Goodbye and good luck.'

Jackson saluted and followed the aide.

CHAPTER FIVE

Overseas Bound

On board the crowded ship, Jackson selected a meeting place for his squad. It was under the bow of the port for'ard lifeboat. Jackson shared a cabin with three other officers. The NCOs cleverly bunked in a store of horse fodder, leaving the troopers to find their own sleeping places, which they did successfully. They slept in a storeroom. The ship was crammed with soldiers and horses. Such is war and its demand on men and horses.

The ship's meals were basic but filling. Feeding the horses was very time consuming even with the help of the soldiers. The soldiers enjoyed working with the horses. It was a distraction from the boredom of doing nothing of consequence day after day.

The horses' areas were hosed out daily with sea water before feeding and watering them. Inspecting the horses was not easy. At times they climbed over the backs of the horses. Some probably missed inspection for a few days.

Eventually the P.T.I.'s began morning exercises. Most accepted the physical routine and began to get fitter and sleep more soundly.

The P.T.I.'s stood on the hastily installed merchant ship gun sponsons for everyone to see them. Even the officers joined in the daily jumping, running on the spot and deep breathing exercises. The exercises took thirty minutes and were completed thirty minutes before breakfast, allowing time for a quick shower. A healthy body and a healthy appetite in the sea air.

The ship sailed in convoy non-stop to Colombo. They stayed there for two days allowing everyone time to go ashore to buy souvenirs or go sightseeing to the inland city of Kandy or do both. It was a beautiful tropical island with greenery everywhere. Some officers were given a tour of the spectacular tea plantations up in the hills.

They then sailed onto Africa and Arabia. The trip through the Red Sea and Suez Canal was most picturesque. The sunsets were spectacular with a red glow shining on the distant desert horizon. The canal started at Port Suez and finished at Port Said, a distance of one hundred and twenty miles. It's a slow trip as the ships are limited to speeds of between eight and fifteen knots to protect the canal walls from the waves washing away the embankment soil. It took a ship around eleven to sixteen hours to complete the trip, provided it did not have to join the queue at Ismalia.

Halfway along the canal is the town of Ismalia on the western shore of a large lake called Lake Timsah. Often ships would have to wait days for their turn as the canal is only one ship wide. When they reached Ismalia there were over a dozen ships waiting to proceed up the Suez Canal. For some unknown reason their ship jumped the queue, and they sailed on without delay.

When the ship arrived at Port Said and the locals saw the Australian flag waving in the breeze, the soldiers on board knew Australians had been there before. Shouts came across the water "Ned Kelly bastards".

When a previous Australian ship had anchored there, local souvenir sellers had blocked the ship's ladder, not allowing access for the ship's crew to go ashore and return. They refused to move clear and away from the ship. The bosun warned them several times to move. When they continued to block the ladder's access, the bosun ordered the duty gangway crew to spray them with the fire hose. Several boats were overturned. Souvenirs and the sellers ended up in the harbour water yelling and screaming abuse. Since then, all ships flying the Australian flag had been greeted with the shouts "Ned Kelly bastards" echoing across the harbour waters.

Unloading the horses was of concern for the three vets as they were unsure of the condition of all the horses. They heaved a sigh of relief, when out of the hundreds of horses, they only lost six. They did not have time to check out why they died but unceremoniously dumped them overboard. Not one Waler died.

The Australian soldiers' first sight of the Sphinx and the pyramids was an eye opener to all of them. The sheer size of the monuments in the never-ending desert was difficult to comprehend, as was the history behind these timeless stone artifacts.

Prior to commencing intense training for the Syria Campaign, an officers' group photograph was organised at the main pyramid. The soldiers heard of it and soon hundreds of them climbed the pyramid and were included in the officers' photograph.

Jackson's team heard of it and joined the rush. Jackson missed out; he was in Syria being briefed. All went well until afterwards when several soldiers were injured climbing down the uneven stones. The photograph became famous and synonymous with the history of Australians at war. It was typical of the larrikin behaviour of the Aussies.

After weeks at sea, Cairo was a town which offered the soldiers wine, women and song. Bars offered all three. Most soldiers acted responsibly; a minority did not.

Some associated with the wrong women and were sent back to Australia for treatment and others drank too much of the local alcohol and caused fights. The majority behaved responsibly and went sightseeing or purchased souvenirs, enjoying the bartering with the Egyptian sellers.

The Australian army had established barracks adjacent the Sphinx. The soldiers were now being trained ready for embarkation to Gallipoli as replacements for the troopers already there. They went on long marches, they drilled and practised mock battles. They were taught how to use the bayonet effectively and to shoot straight.

Jackson's squad was not exempt from field training. They participated in the route marches and war games. They found them very realistic. Soldiers were sometimes wounded by their own. It was then that the soldiers were grateful for the P.T.I.'s exercises. The heat was oppressive with very little natural shade available. Water was at a premium. The troops soon learnt the value of full water bottles and water bags for themselves and their horses.

Rightly or wrongly, discipline was always going to be challenged by Australian soldiers. In the Australian officers' mess one night, an officer told the story of a new British subaltern in his spick and span uniform who walked past a group of Australian soldiers digging some latrines without their shirts on. One soldier was leaning on a shovel and, greeted the subaltern with a cheerful "G'day mate".

The subaltern stopped and said, 'Aren't you forgetting something?'

The soldier asked, 'No, what?'

'A salute,' he said.

The soldier replied, 'Fair go, mate. Are you serious?'

The subaltern then asked, 'Who is in charge here?'

A soldier standing at the back walked slowly forward, while putting on his shirt – with major's insignias. He then said, 'Lieutenant, there are two things you can do for me.'

The Lieutenant asked, 'What are they, sir?'

'First, you can salute me and second – you can bugger off.'

The subaltern saluted and walked away, red-faced, his ears ringing from the laugher of the other Australian soldiers.

Colonel Hewlett was an original Light Horse officer. Tall, slim and straight, he immediately commanded respect. He invited the three vets to be seated and asked his batman for tea to be served. After thanking them for the way they had tended their cargo of horses, he came straight to the point. 'You are still members of the Light Horse regiment, even if you are unattached, but we have a need for a squad to go to Gallipoli. I need to know if the work horses are all still needed there.

'Lieutenant Calsone, as you and your squad seem to have exceptional knowledge of horses, I have selected your squad to go there. Collectively, you and your men seem to have unique skills that have been recognised from above. The other two squads will have duties here for the time being. You other two gentlemen are dismissed. Lieutenant Carlsone, please remain.' The other vets left, closing the door behind them.

The colonel said, 'You are to go Gallipoli and see what value the army is getting from these remaining horses. It appears that most commanders find them unsuitable to haul cannons etc. in the hilly terrain. I am not prepared to waste any more time on these valuable horses or tie up soldiers' productive time when these soldiers could be deployed elsewhere. I have been unable to get a satisfactory answer to my repeated requests for accurate reports on the situation.' He paused. 'Gallipoli is a disaster. I need to know the number of animals - horses, donkeys and mules and their usefulness. As a breeder and a buyer, I want you to decide whether they should be returned to Egypt, shot or left there for army use. You will only be answerable to the beach commander – Major Jones. These are your written orders. I want you and your squad back here before Christmas. Good luck.'

Jackson briefed his team and asked for comments. Only the sergeant spoke. 'I've heard Gallipoli is pretty tough. We'll earn our pay.'

They sailed two days later from Cairo. The ship was packed with soldiers and equipment. As they left the harbour, Jackson wondered what it would be like. At the camp in Egypt, they had heard horrific stories. Were they true or exaggerated? They would soon find out.

Jackson was talking with his team when the sergeant commented.

'The worst thing about being unattached is you have a sense of not belonging. Yes, we know we're needed. I believe we're appreciated, and we do a good job and are respected. But I would prefer to be in a regiment. No disrespect to you, sir. You're probably one of the best officers I've served under.'

Jackson nodded in agreement. 'Yes, you're correct. I feel the same way, but we're being treated as if we're unique. Look at what we've achieved and experienced over the last months, and now we're off into another unknown. Let's hope the situation isn't as bad as we're led to believe and that we all survive and eventually join a regiment.'

CHAPTER SIX

The Army Nurse

Two months after Jackson joined the Australian Army, Mary decided to become a nurse. She joined a large regional hospital which had a medical training department that provided complete training for a nursing career. Her course combined full time technical tuition and practical experience there at the hospital. She enjoyed the challenges and fortunately rose to the occasion. The theory part required considerable study, but her powers of comprehension enabled her to successfully pass all her written examinations with good to very good grades. The practical training she selected was in the emergency ward, rather than general nursing. Although it was difficult at first to accept and handle the sight of major traumas from farm accidents with mechanical vehicles and gun mistakes, she soon adapted. If she knew the injured person, it was a little more difficult to handle. She was an above average student, and the emergency doctors gave her good reports. After two years of intensive study and training, she was classed as a qualified nurse. She realised that she would need more experience and superior qualifications to be classed as a nursing sister.

After her training was completed, she joined the Australian Army Nursing Service. She often met up with Jane and Michael to discuss old times, new times and generally just chat. She noticed a closeness was developing between them. Was it a healthy relationship or was it a recipe for disaster in the future? During her study years, she had returned home on some weekends to see her parents and had very little time to spend with her school day friends, but obviously they had been meeting each other. She had written several times to Jackson telling him of her nursing progress; she expected to be posted overseas soon.

As expected, her posting came through. As presumed, she was off to Cairo initially. After tearful goodbyes with her parents and the best wishes from Jane and Michael for a safe return, she reported to the matron at the army hospital.

The matron read her training details and saw that her trauma experience was far superior to any other new nurse. She commented, 'You will be an asset in a frontline battalion, but you'll probably need to spend some time in a UK rehabilitation hospital to learn army procedures before going to France.'

Mary was given written orders to proceed to the SS Euripides at Port Melbourne and report to Matron Hutton. The ship was scheduled to sail within twenty-four hours.

The dock at Port Melbourne was a hive of activity – cargo being loaded, soldiers marching up the gangway, sailors busy checking people boarding, such as nurses and some others not in uniform.

After having her name ticked off the passenger list, she was shown to a mess deck and waited until she met with Matron Hutton. After a quick chat, Mary was shown to a cabin crammed with bunks. A friendly face, pointed and said, 'Take that one, it's still free.' They introduced each other, as Mary and Anne. Anne was from Western Australia, also a new nurse. Both were of a similar age and excited to be travelling overseas to exotic new countries.

The ship sailed on time and the two nurses stood with many of the others watching Melbourne slowly disappear on the vanishing horizon. They headed out into Bass Strait and turned west, bound for Fremantle for a short stop, before heading north to Colombo in Ceylon. It was one ship in a small convoy of ships of all sizes with warships slipping between them. U-boats and German Raiders were of concern in the vast Indian Ocean. Several merchant ships had been lost and presumed sunk.

These ships had simply vanished without a trace. Some had radioed that they were being shelled by an identified ship. Then radio silence.

The seas were calm with the clouds keeping the sun at bay. It was enjoyable to stand at the guard rails and feel the breeze on one's face. It was serene listening to the water rushing by the ship's side. Sometimes a flying fish would zoom across the waves a foot or so into the air, skimming over the water. Several times they saw dolphins swimming and diving across the bows. They even saw whales in the distance. They watched these mammals frolicking like children, creating huge splashes when they dropped back into the sea.

After a while life at sea became monotonous, until one evening. The alarms and sirens began making a terrible din. An unidentified ship had been sighted on the horizon.

Immediately two destroyers sped off, heading to intercept the unknown vessel. The vessel headed away at speed. The destroyers eventually returned to their scouting stations. Their priority was to protect the convoy. The excitement was brief and soon monotony returned.

A day in Colombo allowed Mary and Anne to carry out some souvenir shopping and sightseeing at the tea plantation up in the hills. The hill country was cool and refreshing after shipboard life.

They proceeded to the entry of the Red Sea where the city of Aden was situated at the south-eastern corner of Arabia. It was an unimpressive city seeming to comprise only square block buildings all the same sandy colour. The ship did not stop and continued travelling up the Red Sea which was a delightful experience with its magnificent sunsets.

The skyline was red when the sun was setting over the Ethiopian Desert and in the morning the sun rose over the Arabian Desert, heralding a bright new sunny day. The Red Sea was a photographer's dream. They soon reached Port Suez, the entrance to the Suez Canal. They sailed slowly up the canal at a reduced speed to avoid washing away the sides of the canal.

Halfway up the canal, the ship came to a large lake at Ismailia and waited their turn in the queue to enter the northern section of the canal. After a further sixty odd miles they reached Port Said.

Between Colombo and Cairo, the nurses attended lectures and treated some soldiers for general ailments such as influenza, gastric upsets, and boils. Some injuries were sustained when soldiers fell down the ship's ladders in rough seas.

Mary and Anne did some private joint medical study to help pass the time. It would stand them in good stead in the months ahead.

Some evenings they sat on the ship's bollards and chatted with the soldiers. Some were feeling lonely and just wanted to chat about home and their wives or girlfriends. The time passed more pleasantly with these meetings.

Mary and Anne were lonely, too. They wrote letters to their families. Anne had a fiancé. Mary wrote to Michael and Jane. She even wrote to Jackson twice. She was aware of the expected delays associated with receiving answers from any of her friends.

She posted five letters upon arriving in Cairo and hoped for an answer to the three letters she had posted in Perth. Luck was with her. Three letters were waiting for her. Her mother, Jane and Michael had each responded.

After finding a quiet spot behind a lifeboat. She read her mother's letter first. It was, as expected, about family, the farm and how they missed her; comforting news but not exciting. Jane's letter was similar but somewhat vague. She wrote as if she was thinking and putting down her thoughts. She mentioned Michael but not Jackson, which Mary found odd.

Jane said she was missing Jackson terribly and, on occasion, met with Michael at the local Saturday dance. She was finding life boring. Looking after her mother and tending to the management of the farm occupied much of her time. She was going for horse rides to help fill in her day. At night she listened to the radio and often fell asleep in her lounge chair.

Michael's letter was full of enthusiasm. He and his father had decided to open up another leather manufacturing business in Melbourne. They had mortgaged the Riverbank property to purchase the business in Melbourne. He would manage the Riverbank workshop, manufacturing and selling saddles, bridles, etc. His parents were confident he could manage the mortgage and the business with a young lad as an assistant.

Although he and Mary were only friends, nothing more, they still felt comfortable corresponding with each other. Mary was pleased he now had an objective in life. At times she sensed he felt rather lost. Now with business responsibilities and challenges, he seemed much more content. Mary quietly shed a few tears. She missed home and her friends. Quietly she folded the letters, put them in her pocket, stood up, wiped away her tears, pulled her shoulders back and walked to the mess deck for a cup of tea.

The matron welcomed the twenty new nurses to Egypt and spoke to each individually, noting their nursing experience. With Mary, she commented about her two years of casualty-emergency experience. Most of the other nurses had worked mainly in general wards, including Anne. The matron continued, 'The following five nurses have been posted to the hospital ship at Gallipoli.' Mary and Anne's names were on the list.

They were both excited and, at the same time, a little apprehensive of the unknown before them. The named nurses were to embark with the replacement troops.

There was a hive of activity on the ship heading to Gallipoli. Soldiers embarked via the rear gangway and officers and nurses used the forward gangway. When the ship sailed from Cairo, the upper deck was crowded with soldiers. There was no cheering. Some had been to Gallipoli before and knew what to expect. Others had been wounded and were returning after rehabilitation in the UK. The rest were just wondering what war was like. They would soon know!

They could hear the Navy vessels' heavy guns firing before they saw the ships. Smoke could be seen in the distance. Then the salvo stopped. A soldier standing nearby said to nobody in particular. 'They'll be leaving the trenches now to advance into – who knows what?'

Mary and Anne were disembarked onto a small Navy work boat and taken to the hospital ship. From the ship, they could see the Gallipoli Peninsula in the distance. The wind carried the sounds of gunfire and smoke in their direction. The five nurses stood on the deck mesmerised by the sight.

A loud voice called to them. 'Nurses, come here, if you please.' It was another matron. She took them to a small cabin with six bunks – three tiers. 'You toss for who sleeps where. Not that you will probably get much sleep. We're very short staffed and we're glad you've finally arrived. I'll be back in an hour, and I'll show you around the ship and introduce you to your peers and doctors.'

The ship looked old and rusty. It smelt of diesel fumes and had the hospital smell Mary knew so well.

The matron said, 'Be aware that this is not the Sydney General Hospital and be prepared for sights which may shock you. But at all times remember to control your emotions. If you can't speak, just nod. You will soon see what I mean.' The new nurses looked at each other but did not say a word.

The ship had wards on the upper decks mainly for improved ventilation and ease of access for patients to be moved. The first two wards were filled with around one hundred patients each and they had only two nurses per ward on duty. These patients were mainly ill, rather than injured, generally caused by the poor hygienic conditions the soldiers lived in when they were in the trenches. Lung problems were prevalent – influenza, asthma, bronchitis and pneumonia mainly. Other soldiers, who had endured gas attacks, also had breathing and eyesight problems.

The next two wards were for soldiers who were wounded by bullets, explosions, etc. Their wounds varied from blindness, amputations of limbs, major body wounds, burns, and skin infections. This was a very demanding ward due to the number of dressing changes required around the clock.

Another ward was for soldiers who had mental problems. Some had been buried alive, others had seen their mates killed in front of them by shrapnel from exploding grenades and bombs. Some cases were called "shell shock" but some doctors would not accept this term. These cases were in limbo!

Her first night on duty, she was by herself for the last two hours of her duty watch, covering the mentally ill ward. She had been advised that normally the early morning duty watch was quiet as most patients were sedated and asleep.

One patient started having nightmares and began screaming and tearing his head bandages off. Mary was unable to calm him or physically control him. Two duty deck watch sailors heard her call for help and came to her aid. They held him down until he became calm. Mary then managed to have him drink a strong sedative. Within ten minutes he was asleep. The next day, a doctor approached her and complimented her on her calmness during the handling of the potentially dangerous incident.

Mary told him the sailors controlled him, not her and she continued to answer him, by saying, 'There could have been a very different result without them.'

The doctor nodded and acknowledged that all the medical sections were short of numbers. In future, he would try to always have two nurses on duty each duty shift.

Mary handled the sight of the badly wounded without any trouble but there was so much to do, she was exhausted when she finished each shift.

Mary and Anne often compared notes when they met after duty shift.

They agreed, although they were performing demanding nursing tasks and working long hours, that they also felt rewarded with their contribution in assisting the Australian soldiers during the war.

Both Mary and Anne were due to be posted to an English rehabilitation hospital. Shortly before their transfer came through, a particularly ugly incident occurred involving Anne.

Late one evening, when everyone was starting to settle down for the night, Anne was walking past a shell-shocked soldier. Normally, he was composed and reserved, and kept to himself. This night he was agitated. Anne had previously sat by his bunk, chatting to him about home.

He suddenly jumped up and grabbed Anne by the arm and hugged her, calling her 'mother'. Anne struggled and called for help. Some soldiers saw this and with others, began to run towards them. He then dragged Anne out of the ward and onto the main deck. He called out, 'Don't come near me or my mother or we will jump.' Several others had come out of the ward. All went quiet, waiting to see what he would do next. It was an unpredictable situation.

The Navy officer of the watch looked down from the bridge and, without thinking, shouted to some nearby sailors, 'Don't just stand there, rescue that nurse and restrain that man.' The soldier holding Anne looked up at him and then calmly jumped over the side into the dark sea waters, taking a screaming Anne with him.

The officer then ordered, 'Away lifeboat.' A sailor was about to dive over the side, when the officer of the watch, shouted. 'Leave the rescue to the boat crew.' The sailor stopped but a walking patient dived over the side and after a minute or so managed to locate and grab hold of a gasping Anne. The lifeboat lifted them from the sea, but the soldier was not found. The boat crew rowed around in the dark area for thirty minutes but did not locate his body. He was reported as "Presumed drowned."

The officer of the watch met the lifeboat. He said to the patient who saved Anne, 'When I give an order, it will be obeyed.' The patient turned and quietly replied, 'I'm Australian Light Horse and I only answer to my officers.'

The Navy officer turned and walked away without saying a word. The soldier was then led away by two nurses for a change of pyjamas and a hot cup of tea to the cheers of the surrounding audience of patients, nurses and sailors.

That was not the end of the unfortunate saga. Whenever the Royal Navy officer appeared on deck, the Australian soldiers turned their backs to him. He was transferred to another ship within the month.

As a sequel to this inciden, the drama had been witnessed by an Australian officer who recommended the rescuer be "mentioned in despatches" for saving the life of the Australian nurse.

Anne was none the worse for her ordeal and was as bright as a button within a day or two and resumed her normal duties. Two weeks later they were on their way to England. Their posting to the hospital ship had been an experience of a lifetime.

They were stories to be told to their grandchildren – the horrific wounds they saw, the harrowed looks on the faces of mentally affected, the stoic bravery of men who knew they were dying. Apart from what they saw, there were the stories they heard when siting with them, listening to them talk about the horrors out on the battlefields and living in the trenches.

At times the nurses would mentally switch off and just nod, as advised by the wise matron. They found it better not to ask questions. These sad memories would stay with Mary and Anne for their lifetime.

CHAPTER SEVEN

Gallipoli

At Cairo, Jackson and his squad boarded a heavily loaded troop ship for the first time, without their horses. They still wore the distinctive Light Horse uniform, together with the emu feather in their slouch hat. But probably not for much longer!

The sea voyage was pleasant, calm seas and plenty of sunlight. They slept on deck on empty canvas bags. The soldiers were quick and had claimed all the good spots. Mess time was a struggle; the queue was halfway around the ship's lower deck. The lavatories or heads had long queues, too. Although most of the soldiers peed from the ship's side – after first checking the wind direction. The ones who didn't soon learnt!

The squad saw and heard the heavy navy ships firing repeated salvos into the hills of the peninsula, just as they first saw Gallipoli on the horizon. The closer they came to land, the more activity there was on the ship.

Jackson and his squad would be one of the last groups to disembark. The soldiers were all loaded with their kit and arms and queued in line as ordered by their NCOs. The sailors were busy readying their work boats to embark the soldiers.

As they came closer to the beaches, the multitude of sounds was now increasing. The crack of rifle fire, accompanied by machine gun bursts, together with shell explosions and smoke, were a chilling warning of what they were to expect.

The soldiers had now boarded the workboats. A small armada of them headed for the beach head. They soon came under gun fire from the hills. It was inevitable some soldiers would be killed or wounded before they reached the beach. When they landed, they immediately ran across to the beach cliff face. Many soldiers did not make the safety of the cliff face.

The workboats quickly turned back to their ship. It was now Jackson's squad's turn to go ashore. They each shook hands wishing each other good luck and to meet wherever Major Jones was. The workboat was as basic as its name. It was seaworthy but just an open shell with two navy seamen as crew, a helmsman and a for'ard hand.

The for'ard hand said, 'Get ready. We'll be in five feet of water soon and that's where you get off – and quickly. I don't like being shot at several times a day. Ready. Jump now!'

Jackson jumped expecting to touch the sand with his head out of the water, but he went under water a foot or so. He had his legs bent. When he straightened up, his head was above water as he waded towards the beach. He and his squad managed to stay together, even after the panicked run across the sand. He heard a few zips as bullets flew past him. Fortunately, his squad was unscathed. When they reached the safety of the cliff face, they looked back and saw bodies falling to the sand. As it was still daylight, they could expect no help for several hours.

Major Jones was a difficult man to find. Yes, he had an office of sorts, a well-used old tent but a passing soldier advised them he was rarely there, as he was a very busy man. They decided to wait there for him to return. It would be senseless for them to even try to locate him; Gallipoli was a shambles. The gunfire never let up. They were surprised at seeing so many wounded soldiers continuing to move down to the beach, in a never-ending stream.

Jackson's curiosity was aroused when he saw a soldier leading a donkey carrying a wounded soldier. He watched the soldier with the donkey as the medicos carried the soldier into a tent.

As the man with the donkey came by, Jackson asked the soldier, 'What do you think of the use of horses here?'

The soldier replied, 'Well, the bigger they are, the less use they are in the gullies and valleys. The smaller the horse or mule, or donkey or whatever, the more surefooted they are. I've lost count of the number of trips I've done with this donkey. The draught horses are useless. They brought them over to tow cannons. In this terrain? Utter stupidity.'

Jackson asked, 'What are your thoughts on the medium size horse?'

'Take them back to Egypt. They're not much good for the Light Horse here, but they would be good for towing ambulances and light cannon in France.'

He asked, 'Are there many here?'

'The horses are at the beach behind that small cliff,' the soldier answered.

'One last question. What do you feed your donkey on?'

'I feed my mate food scraps and ground-up bush shrub,' the soldier said. 'I must away. Duty calls.' He waved and walked back to the gunfire area up and over the steep hill.

Jackson heard the sergeant call him. Turning, he saw the elusive Major Jones. He walked towards a smiling middle-aged man.

'Welcome, Lieutenant Carlsone. I see you have started your assessment already. The donkey man is a good judge of horse flesh and believes we don't need all of them over here. However, that is your assignment. I will help you where I can.'

They shook hands and retired to the major's tent office. He also slept there. This was his kingdom even though it only had a desk, a bunk bed and two chairs. A self-made rack was his wardrobe. It was lean, clean and dry – no mud!

Jackson started by asking, 'How many horses are there on Gallipoli?'

The major replied, 'We have hundreds and hundreds of donkeys and mules. Only a few draught horses and around a thousand standard or so horses at the beach. There are no Walers.

'Many more horses are up in the Frontline and are needed there. Some horses have wandered off and are now with the Turks. Others are in poor health due to the inadequate food available. A few are sick and I was about to put them down. When I heard you were coming, I decided to wait. I would suggest you visit the paddocks. It will answer most of your other questions.'

Jackson called the sergeant and told him to take charge of the squad. He would take the corporal with him to inspect the horses.

The three men walked close to the cliff face to avoid any rifle fire from the Turks. When they got to the paddock, they saw that the horses were a sorry lot. They were standing in groups, their heads down. Their coats were dull and dusty and their eyes dull.

Jackson approached them, but they hardly moved. It was obvious that they had not been cared for or worked. The inspection took nearly all day.

The major had been correct – several horses needed to be put down.

When he told the major, he nodded and said, 'I know this may shock you, but I need to tell the supply officer. Meat is scarce here, and horse flesh is part of our food source.'

He continued, 'If you are happy that the flesh from these horses is suitable for human consumption, a butcher will be sent to be on hand when the horses are put down.'

Jackson nodded. 'I've inspected the sick horses and I can see no reason that the horse flesh could not be used for human consumption, particularly if the meat is fresh and well cooked.' While he was little surprised at the major's question, it was a reasonable one. Fresh horse meat would be a delicacy for the troops in a war zone. In several European countries during this war, horse meat was being sold for human consumption to the general public.

Jackson and the corporal had not expected so many horses to be held here. They decided to inspect the entire herd prior to any slaying.

It came to Jackson's attention that many hundreds of horses had been sent to Gallipoli but had not been allowed to disembark and were carried on to the UK.

It appeared these facts had not been advised to the Central Control Area.

The remaining horses were all under-fed but otherwise they were in reasonable condition. Jackson now had the unenviable task of shooting the sick horses. There were only three beyond help.

He had performed this task several times, but he still didn't like killing animals, even when it was humane. He positioned his revolver barrel between the horse's eyes and pulled the trigger. Immediately the horse fell down dead. Four soldiers began cutting off the tail and the hoofs complete with shoes. They then proceeded to skin the animal after removing the gut and then cut out large meat sections.

Only the prime cuts such as flanks, shoulders and ribs were taken away by the cookhouse team. The remainder of the carcases were tossed into the sea.

The skins would be scraped and laid over an ants' nest to remove any remaining flesh. Fat from the boiled meat would then be rubbed into the skin, making it soft and pliable.

Jackson wondered, *are these the lucky four soldiers to receive a warm blanket each?*

The hoofs would be used to make glue and the hair was good for sutures.

The draught horses were a problem. They were too big and heavy to hoist onto a work boat. Jackson felt it would be more humane to drive them into the Turks' area. Perhaps they would end up as farm horses. The donkeys and the mules would stay on Gallipoli. The number of horses to remain would be agreed between the major and Jackson. Teams like the soldier and the donkey were definitely needed. His logic helped Jackson make his first decision.

The donkeys and mules would stay at Gallipoli, along with a select number of the fittest and most healthy horses. After selecting the surplus horses, the squad then moved them into a holding paddock to be shipped out of Gallipoli.

The horses were in demand in other war zones, making them valuable. The horses not required at Gallipoli would be transported to Egypt, where their future destination would be decided.

On their trip to the beach, Jackson noticed that the work boats were fitted with a large hoist. After asking around he was advised that work boat hoists had been fitted to lift field guns and could definitely lift a horse. When he discussed this idea with the major, he nodded and said it could be done. There was a small beach with deep water and the area was not in the Turkish offensive area.

His plan was to fit the horses with a sling, then make them swim a short distance by pulling them into the water from the shore to the work boat. Using the hoist, they would hook the canvas sling, and hoist each horse up onto the work boat and then onto the ship.

The major contacted the Navy. They advised that a cargo ship was due to arrive within a fortnight and the ship's captain had been advised of the horse cargo.

Jackson assembled his squad and sent them out to find any remains of written off tents suitable to make slings. They eventually located sufficient material to make twenty slings. They used the straps previously used to lift the field guns, to complete the slings.

The horses were at the beach the day before the ship was due to arrive. They had tested the slings with a sturdy rope and two block and tackles and a tree. No one knew where the block and tackles came from. They found the slings did not antagonise the horses; they just hung there quietly looking around.

Under the cover of darkness, six work boats unloaded their cargo first and then returned to within a hundred feet from the shore. A line was heaved by a sailor and attached to the horse's head strap ring. The horse was then dragged into the seawater and made to swim towards the workboat. When it was alongside, the hoist hook was clipped onto the sling by a sailor and the horse was slung aboard. He then secured the horse in the workboat and the hoisting was repeated at the ship. The slings were removed and then sent back to the beach. They carried twenty horses at a time in the work boats. They worked all night with the plan going quickly and smoothly.

Only one horse was lost when the sling broke and the horse hit the ship's guard rail and fell into the sea, obviously in pain. The horse was badly injured, and a soldier humanely shot it.

The ship's captain was pleased with the planning and implementation of the shipment and advised Colonel Hewlett of it.

After the horses' assessment project had been completed, Jackson and his squad had expected to return to Egypt.

After he had completed his written report to Colonel Hewlett, he reported to Major Jones, who informed him, he and his squad were needed in Gallipoli for a little longer.

Jackson and his squad received the news without concern. After all they were Light Horse soldiers.

Major Jones introduced him to Lieutenant Wills who was to be his advisor and his mentor. Wills had been an original arrival at Gallipoli. He had a dour look and was rather lean but looked to be tough and determined.

He greeted Jackson with a handshake and a nod and said abruptly, 'If we leave now, we will be at our post before sunset.'

Jackson and his team followed him. In single file they walked up and down gullies. Eventually entering a cleared area overlooking the Allies' camps.

Wills took Jackson aside. 'I'm not happy about being a nurse-maid to some horse minders, but if you do as I tell you, we'll get on fine.'

Jackson replied angrily, 'I will work with you but not for you. However, I do respect your greater experience.'

Wills looked at him and laughed. 'I like your answer. We'll get on fine.'

The next day Wills took Jackson and the sergeant up to the Frontline.

'Make sure you remember this track, or else you'll end up either dead or a prisoner of war.' They came to a ridge and crawled up to look over the major battlefield.

It consisted of hundreds and hundreds of shell holes, barbwire and worst of all – bodies. Smoke wafted over the entire vista, making the scene seem unreal with rifle fire, machine guns bursting, grenades exploding and soldiers advancing from trenches, and some falling.

Looking to the right, Jackson could see trenches angled in all directions, more barbwire, more soldiers and some tents. It appeared to be utter shambles. He could see a first aid post with wounded soldiers lying on the ground waiting to be treated. This was war.

The sergeant looked at Jackson, trying to gauge his reaction to his first exposure of the carnage of war.

Jackson returned his look. 'Well, we're here now.'

Jackson's squad was given the task of patrolling a strategic observation point and to report any unusual activity. The position overlooked a deep long valley. The Turks had a base at the far end. Sometimes they sent three of four soldiers a short distance up the valley. Even though they were of no real concern, their movements needed to be monitored.

Jackson split his team into two. The sergeant and the acting corporal had one half of the squad with the corporal and he the other half.

After a few boring days, they saw a bit of activity in the valley. Three Turks were moving further up the valley than normal. Jackson decided to see where they might be heading. Accompanied by a trooper, he cautiously walked down the valley about a hundred yards. When he turned a blind corner, he saw a Turk standing ten feet away, holding a rifle. Two other Turks were sitting on the ground smoking.

Startled, Jackson instinctively drew his revolver and fired at the standing Turk. The bullet hit his rifle butt spinning it from his hands. The Turk immediately surrendered, raising his arms. The other two, who remained seated, also surrendered.

Jackson was shaken at what had happened in a split second. The corporal had his rifle pointed menacingly at the Turks. When Jackson gained his composure, he motioned the three captives to walk back up the track to the Allies' observation position. The Turks did not seem to be concerned at being captured and said little to each other. They gave no trouble and walked back as directed. The corporal collected their rifles and slung them over his shoulder.

They arrived back as the sergeant's men were coming up to change over.

The sergeant congratulated him. 'I wish I could be there to see the look on Lieutenant Wills' face.'

When Jackson and his men reached the beach with the prisoners, work came to a standstill. Few had seen Turkish prisoners.

Lieutenant Wills looked at Jackson and shook his head. 'Well, I'll be buggered. I misjudged you and your men.'

An intelligence officer soon arrived and, after asking Jackson to send him a written report within twenty-four hours, he took the prisoners away. When the story got around about him shooting the rifle from the Turk's hands, even the officer commanding the Australian soldiers was impressed. Jackson and his corporal were the talk of the week.

Jackson sat on the beach and thought over what had happened.

Was it instinct that made him draw his revolver and fire it at the Turk or was it shear panic? It had all happened so fast and was over in less than a minute, although it seemed to be much longer. Would he react the same if a similar incident happened again?

They continued the same observation duties for another two weeks and were then deployed to the Front. The battle noise and the conditions were difficult to accept at first but after a few days it became accepted as the norm.

Jackson was called upon to help the medicos. As a vet he had plenty of experience sewing the two sides of deep cuts together on horses. At times he performed this surgery on soldiers without a doctor being present. He had proven capable and that was sufficient qualification with the current shortage of qualified staff and the carnage that was occurring on the battlefield only a few hundred yards away. Often a spent stray bullet reached the temporary casualty tent.

At the Front, the rifle and machine gunfire continued throughout the day. Allied grenades were tossed to the enemy and the Turks threw ones back to them. The soldiers used homemade periscopes to look for the Turks without having to expose themselves.

Jackson's squad was reassigned to a surveillance post. The post had an assigned sniper who had already shot three Turks. He just nodded when the sergeant and the others arrived.

They were overlooking a long gully with heavy undergrowth. The sniper pointed to a tall tree. They waited for half an hour. He took aim and fired. A moment later a Turkish soldier fell to the ground – dead.

The sniper said, 'We've had their snipers killing our troops, so my commander told me to find them and kill them. I've got four so far. I used to be a dingo hunter, so I'm a fairly good shot.' He then picked up his very powerful binoculars and started looking again.

The sniper, the sergeant and his troopers came under fire when a small group of Turkish soldiers crept up the valley under darkness. Fortunately, an alert trooper who was on night watch, heard a noise like a twig breaking. He fired in that direction and received several answering shots from the Turks. The shots had the others awake and they began firing at the flashes of the Turkish rifle bullets. The exchange of gunfire was only short. Once the Turks realised they had been discovered, they retreated back down the valley.

The next day, the squad had their baptism of fire. A short excursion to the area where the Turks had been, revealed a large quantity of blood. Obviously, one of them had wounded a Turk.

The rest of the time they were on surveillance became boring until they were ordered to proceed down the valley and see if any Turks were still in the area. The sergeant put two men on forward point duty as scouts to report back if they spotted any activity. The rest of his team spread out in twos. The undergrowth helped them to move under cover, but it was difficult to remain quiet with broken branches on the ground. After two hours the scouts came back.

One scout had come upon a large, deserted camp site. He said it appeared to have been vacated several days ago. The sergeant and the other troopers visited the deserted camp site and they agreed with the scout.

When the sergeant went back to Command and gave his report. He found a change of direction had occurred.

Major Jones came to see Lieutenant Carlsone with the news that he and his squad were being posted to England and were to travel on the next passing ship. Jackson was handed his orders. He was relieved they had received this news, as he and his squad were due to go over the top in two days and they were not looking forward to that ordeal.

Ironically Gallipoli was abandoned the week after they left. From the 15th of December 1915, thirty-six thousand soldiers were successfully removed from

Gallipoli without one death, together with stores, artillery, mules and horses. The evacuation was planned by an Australian officer. Jackson's squad had been in Gallipoli for nearly three months.

They wondered where they would be based to celebrate Christmas 1915. Now that they were moving again, there would be further delays in receiving mail. It was disappointing but that was army life.

CHAPTER EIGHT

England

Jackson continued to write to Jane and Michael. Occasionally, he also wrote to Mary. He enjoyed her light-hearted stories. She made no mention of her onerous duties and the horrendous wounds and injuries she saw. She was an exceptional person. Maybe he would meet her, if she was posted overseas.

Their ship, the S.S. Dunedin, arrived on time and was soon disembarking the relieving soldiers and embarking the soldiers returning to England for a well-earned rest. The ship sailed late the same day. It was part of a convoy formed due to the activity of German U-boats in the Mediterranean Sea.

The cargo ships were scattered but close to each other and protected by destroyers zipping around them.

Jackson and his squad mixed with the soldiers and they could see the strain on their faces. Some spoke of the action they had been through. They listened but did not comment.

Others gave the occasional nod of their head. It seemed better than asking questions. Several times during the voyage, they were woken at night by screams from soldiers enduring nightmares.

The seas were moderate with little wind. The voyage was relaxing except for the constant concern of patrolling U-boats.

Just south of Malta they heard an explosion to their right. The destroyers were soon firing depth charges, their sirens wailing.

Jackson was standing on the ship's bridge talking with the first officer.

On hearing the explosion, the duty officer immediately turned and shouted into a microphone. 'Gun crews to stations. Other crews to readiness.' The captain quickly left the chart room and entered the bridge as the duty officer pointed to the damaged ship.

Jackson could see smoke in the distance. An American ship had been struck amidships by a torpedo. It was a welded hull Liberty ship and they could not sustain torpedo explosion damage as well the British rivetted hull ships.

Through binoculars, Jackson could see the ship was sinking. It was slowly turning on its side. He could see sailors sliding down the sides and swimming away from the sinking ship. He wondered if they could be saved by the Navy.

The convoy was not allowed to stop for any reason. The Navy officer commanding the support flotilla would make that decision when he knew where the submarine was and what damage the depth charges had inflicted.

The destroyers continued firing depth charges. Suddenly, a submarine began surfacing adjacent the S.S. Dunedin.

Jackson watched as the gun crews commenced firing at the submarine. The soldiers returning to UK had a front row seat. The gun crews missed their first three shots, but the fourth shell hit the stern and the submarine stopped moving.

A German officer appeared from the conning tower just as a destroyer loomed alongside the submarine. It soon had a boarding party onboard to capture the submarine. The soldiers cheered and clapped.

The action had taken less than an hour. The flotilla commander despatched a destroyer to pick up the survivors of the American ship.

The captain of the S.S. Dunedin received a signal from the fleet admiral with 'A well done'. The signal was framed and kept on the bridge.

Jackson wrote to Jane describing the scene. It was almost like a movie picture, and he was in it. He had started a diary of his experiences and after thoughts. *Maybe, I will write a book some day.* His letters were being heavily censored. Jane could only guess the missing words in the written lines.

Before they reached England, they had two more submarine scares. Periscopes were sighted but the destroyers' depth charges had kept the submarines at bay.

They soon sighted Gibraltar, which was a spectacular large land mass. Positioned at the entrance to the Mediterranean Sea, it was a major strategic military stronghold of the British Army.

The convoy did not stop. It continued to Portsmouth where all and sundry were disembarked. Jackson's orders directed that he and his squad were to proceed to a remount station in the north of England. They were to inspect and select five hundred Walers for a regiment of Light Horsemen who were due to arrive within the next month or so.

They were travelling in uniforms suitable only for the tropics. Snow was on the ground and the air temperature varied between forty and twenty degrees Fahrenheit. They managed to scrounge some woollen underwear from a benevolent charity shop. Being from Australia helped. The women sales ladies went great bundles and enjoyed listening to the twang in their accents.

They travelled to Euston railway station and then to the Romsey Remount Barracks. Fortunately, the trains were warm and each station served hot drinks.

When they arrived, the Romsey Barracks duty officer said, 'We knew of your forthcoming arrival, but we had not been given a date.'

Jackson and the NCOs could be provided with accommodation, but the troopers were a problem. They had a dormitory with beds but no mattresses or linen.

Jackson said, 'I want the duty storeman called and told of our requirements. I'm staying here until my men are provided with sleeping quarters.'

The officer of the watch asked, 'How many troopers do you have?'

Jackson replied, 'Ten.'

The officer of the watch considered for a moment. 'There are twenty Wrens due to arrive next week and their quarters are ready. Use them tonight and I'll note in the daily logbook of the need to have your troop's dormitory ready by 1100 hours tomorrow.

'The NAAFI is still open if you feel like a drink or a cuppa.'

Jackson nodded his thanks and then briefed his squad. Some of his squad went to the NAAFI and with their emu feathers in their hats, they became an instant attraction. Soldiers bought them drinks and then servicewomen began to come over. Some immediately began a very brief relationship.

The next morning, Lieutenant Carlsone reported to the barrack's commander, Colonel Woods, who was an Australian by birth. His parents had returned to England in the 1900's. His father had been a senior member of the British Government.

'Welcome to England, Lieutenant Carlsone. I was wondering when you would arrive. Our communications need to improve. Take a seat.

'I have your orders and I believe they are realistic and achievable.'

Jackson nodded. 'Yes, I have an experienced squad and hopefully we will not have any inclement weather. Do you have a large open space building available? It would help us to assess the riders in dry conditions.'

Colonel Woods nodded. 'We have a drill hall that we use for Passing out Parades in wet weather. We also play various sports inside. Let's go for a walk and I'll show you around. I have an hour to spare this morning. The barracks covers over one hundred and fifty acres. We have six large paddocks with hundreds of horses of all descriptions. We even have some Walers in the herds, or mobs, as you Australians call them,' he commented. 'Tomorrow may be of interest to you. We are testing volunteers for a mounted infantry regiment to be sent to the Suez Canal and into the Sinai Desert.'

Jackson answered, 'Yes, I would like to watch and give my opinion.'

Next morning, Jackson and his sergeant went to the drill hall.

Colonel Woods waved to him from the small rostrum he was using to view the volunteers. There were twenty horses on a picket line.

They were in time to see the volunteers put a saddle on a horse. Several were competent, some marginally so and some thought they knew what to do but didn't. The instructor then stood back and gave a detailed description of how it should be done. He did not demonstrate it physically.

After ten minutes, he ordered, 'Mount up.'

Five riders had their saddle slip, six riders mounted incorrectly. To the successfully mounted riders, he ordered, 'Ride around the circuit once then jump the two hurdles.'

The fifteen remaining riders began trotting. Two more saddles slipped. Thirteen remained mounted and successfully completed the jumps.

The instructor ordered, 'Release the reins and fold your arms and repeat the jumps.'

The thirteen remaining riders satisfactorily completed the jumps without reins.

The instructor asked, 'What did you not do?' No one answered. He continued, 'When you saddle a horse you are unfamiliar with, don't trust the tightness of the girdle. Often horses will expand their chest barrel when they feel the weight of the saddle. Mount the horse and ride for a few minutes and recheck the girth. You may find that the billets will need tightening.'

He addressed the seven riders who did not complete the test. 'Put your saddles on correctly and repeat what you have just observed and please learn to mount a horse correctly. You each have a week to be practise perfect for your next test or else you will not be joining the mounted infantry. Tomorrow you will learn horse care in the field.'

Twice Wounded

Jackson was impressed with the instructor's attitude with the potential recruits.

He noticed one horse that had a saddle slip, was playing up. Jackson went to him.

The instructor said, 'He should not have been here today. We've had trouble with him. I don't think he's been broken in yet.'

Jackson asked, 'Do you mind if I try?'

'No, sir.'

Jackson selected a saddle and blanket and started talking to the horse. He made sure the saddle girth was tight. He tightened it once then waited a minute or two and he was then able to tighten it some more, proving the instructor's point.

Jackson led the horse to the centre of the drill hall and then quickly swung himself into the saddle. The horse immediately started to buck and throw his head around. He twisted and spun but Jackson as a former rodeo buckjumper rider was ready for him.

Jackson had one arm high in the air helping his balance. After about thirty seconds or so, the horse stopped bucking and Jackson had him trotting around the drill hall. The horse was still restless and was throwing his head around, but he now responded to the rider. The watching soldiers clapped his rodeo performance.

The colonel came over. 'Well done. It's made my day. I can see why you're a Light Horseman.'

The instructor came over to them and asked, 'Can I accept he can now be ridden safely?'

Jackson replied, 'Only by an experienced rider. He's a good horse but I'd be watchful of him. Please excuse me, I had better go to work.'

Jackson's first task was to select a few horses for heavy duty. A paddock was selected and then the sorting commenced. He was pleasantly surprised to find a number of Walers.

After inspecting a selected horse, it would be marked with a six-inch diameter green dye dot on the left side of the neck. The squad had worked efficiently and selected their five hundred horses well within the month.

Jackson's squad had all gained valuable horse care experience by watching, listening and asking questions when he was performing veterinary tasks. The entire squad now had exceptional skills in horse care and maintenance.

The squad had been unattached for nearly a year and Jackson wondered how much longer they would remain together.

Captain Lane, with his Australian Army team, arrived three days later. After exchanging pleasantries over tea, Captain Lane handed Lieutenant Carlsone a sealed envelope. It was his next set of orders, plus a promotion to captain. Smiling inwardly, he read the remainder of his orders and to his dismay, it was as he had feared. He and the corporal and three troopers of his selection were to stay at the Romsey Remount Barracks. He had been appointed the officer overseeing horse management standards and they were to be attached to the British Army Standards Unit. He would be briefed further on his assignment by Colonel Woods.

The orders left Jackson with a dilemma – who was to stay and who was to go? He called his team together.

As expected, they did not accept the orders with any enthusiasm. Jackson said, 'This is a decision I feel we should all participate in. Who of you would like to stay in the UK and who would like to go to France?'

Three said they would stay and three voted for France. The other three were undecided, leaving Jackson no choice than to make up their minds for them.

He said, 'Three of you have volunteered to fill the positions in the UK, the remainder of you will be going to France with Sergeant Brown.' They accepted his decision calmly and nodded in agreement.

One final deed needed to be done. 'Corporal, you are promoted to acting sergeant and Trooper Russell, as the senior trooper, you are promoted to acting corporal. Congratulations.' Handshakes all round!

The evening prior to the squad separating, they hired a room at the local pub. The owner excelled himself. The meal was excellent, as was the local beer. They recalled what they had done as a team, even the snake bite incident got a laugh. Jackson stood up and proposed a toast to the King, Australia, the Light Horse Regiments, the squad and last but not least – friends at home.

After the next morning's parade, the seven Light Horsemen mounted a vehicle to take them to a London bound train. Jackson wondered if they would meet again.

The sergeant and his team were stationed at an officers' training base. He was given the task of teaching new officers basic marching drills. He found it difficult. Newly promoted troops from the Front were not a problem but the English so called upper class had difficulty accepting orders from him due to his rank, until a Guards major read the riot act to them. 'I don't care who your father is – obey the sergeant or go!'

They then acted responsibly. Five nurses were new and had trouble co-ordinating arms and legs initially.

One nurse, Jane Joseph, in particular, had trouble relaxing and marching naturally. Sergeant Brown nagged her again and again until she got it right.

At the Passing out Parade, the new officers did their drills excellently. After the parade the sergeant was walking past a doorway when he was called. It was new Lieutenant Joseph.

She said, 'A salute is in order.'

He saluted her and waited for her to say something. She smacked him in the face. 'That's for harassing me.' She then stepped forward and kissed him. 'That's for teaching me to know my left foot from my right.' They both laughed and walked alongside each other back to their respective quarters.

They formed a relationship and met whenever they could get away from the army. They were both in their forties and would never marry. They were too set in their ways, and neither would exchange the countries of their birth. From the short time that they knew each other, they had very pleasant memories. Eventually he and his team were sent to France at short notice. They wrote to each other for a while but did not meet again.

CHAPTER NINE

Unusual Assignment

When Jackson entered Colonel Woods' office, there were two other officers there. The five sat around a table, maps laid out.

The colonel introduced the others as Captain Walsh and Major Main from the British War Office.

Major Main spoke first. 'What I tell you now is confidential within your squad. As you are aware horse meat is now available for human consumption. Coincidently, we are having hundreds, maybe thousands of army horses stolen throughout England. We believe the stealing up north is organised by one group.' The others nodded.

'We need you to find out who is behind this. We want you to be our eyes and ears. You will have perfect cover under your duty statement in your new role.' He paused. 'You will each be sworn in as special constables and each of you will be supplied with a set of civilian clothes. I believe there will times when you will need to dress mufti.'

Jackson sat, listening to and absorbing the words.

The colonel then spoke. 'You will be given the areas where the thefts are occurring. They are mainly in the far north counties, although we are losing horses from all over England. This is a map of the main northern remount stations and where the thefts are occurring. You will depart next Monday. You will be required to send me a weekly report.' He looked up from the map. 'I will be your contact point. As a Justice of the Peace, before you leave, I will swear each of your team in as special constables.' He stood up indicating the meeting was over.

Jackson sat with his small team and told them of the meeting. The task gave the five of them a feeling of excitement. A challenge with a difference!

Two days later they headed to their first destination. They were expected but were greeted apprehensively by the North-eastern Remount Base Commander. He had had troubles in the past when several horses scheduled to be sent to France had been rejected by an army ambulance horse crew because of cracked hoofs. They were small cracks, but the horses could soon have become incapacitated in the muddy conditions in France.

The barracks had known of an impending visit by a specialist horse team, and the commander had been actively inspecting his herds.

Jackson had allowed a fortnight to three weeks for each visit. They planned to spend the morning at the barracks and then wander around the village in the late afternoon.

Dressed as civilians, they would visit shops and pubs in districts where there were plenty of horses. After nearly three weeks they were still without a positive lead.

Casually the team looked for the army arrow brand. The largest butcher in the county was *The Grange*, and it was authorised to sell horse meat. Each time they walked by the butcher shop it had a blue wagon with *The Grange* printed on each side parked in a side lane. Jackson put that in his report.

Over a drink in the mess one night, he mentioned about the horse thefts. The commander replied that none had occurred recently. He felt the thieves had moved on to newer pastures. His guards now carried out patrols at different times each night. Two weeks ago, the night guards had disturbed some possible intruders, but they were unable to intercept them.

After three weeks had gone by, Jackson decided to leave. He thanked the base commander for his assistance and handed him a copy of his report, The commander was delighted his base had been found to be a "most satisfactory" standard. The report detailed the respective areas inspected. A second confidential report was included in relation to his covert operation. With best wishes, a handshake, a salute, Jackson and his squad were off again.

Harrowsgate Remount Base had just been established and Base Commander, Colonel Lock, took affront at being inspected so soon.

After the normal introductions, the base commander, commented: 'Good heavens, we've only been here a dog watch.'

Jackson said, 'We're aware of that and maybe we can assist in some way.'

The commander cooled down and nodded. 'Yes, that's true. We'll see!' The team did a base inspection the next morning and the only item of concern was the positioning of the dispensary.

From a security point of view, it was not within the main administration office block which was permanently guarded. The commander agreed; his aide had pointed it out to him.

They intended to remodel the fodder store and transfer the drugs there and the fodder would be stored in the current dispensary.

A trooper asked Jackson if they could borrow some horses while they were there as they hadn't ridden for quite some time.

Jackson asked the base commander who readily agreed and gave them horses without the military arrow brand.

Jackson's team commenced their visits to the Harrowsgate town, wandering down the main street, looking in windows as would ordinary shoppers, not really knowing what they were looking for.

The town was just another rural town with horses everywhere. Jackson became curious when he saw two horses that he thought looked like Walers. They were hitched outside a general store with blankets on. He strolled over and lifted the lefthand side of the blanket to check the brand. It was not a military brand. However, when he lifted the blanket on the other horse, he saw the military army arrow. Jackson slowly walked over to the sergeant and told him of his find.

They needed to follow the horse but not yet; they needed more than one horse. Their prayers were answered when a *Grange* wagon came around the corner with the two particular horses in tow and headed out of town.

They now had a positive lead. The sergeant walked into the pub and ordered a pint of lager and started chatting with the barmaid.

Casually he asked, 'Which way is it to the *Grange?*'

She replied, pointing, 'It's about ten miles straight down that road. You can't miss it.'

The sergeant quickly left to report to Jackson.

The team rode back to the barracks and sat down to decide what to do next.

A trooper suggested, 'Why don't we watch the comings and goings at the *Grange*. It's going to be difficult catching them stealing the horses, but we can catch them when the horses are delivered, if they are the culprits.'

Jackson nodded and asked each of them, 'Do you have any other ideas or comments?' No one said anything. 'No! Right let's plan around the idea of watching the *Grange*. We need to survey the area, the buildings and exits. The fewer the exits, the easier it will be for us.'

The team was viewing the map of the bases where the horse thefts had occurred. Jackson commented they all had railway sidings within the immediate area.

A trooper pointed and said, 'So does the *Grange*. See, it has a siding close by.'

Jackson nodded and replied, 'Well spotted. I think we'll concentrate on watching their railway siding from now on.'

Jackson decided to send the acting sergeant into the *Grange* establishment, posing as a horse trader. He was to discretely look around and remember as much of the layout of the buildings as possible without making them suspicious.

The acting sergeant rode up the laneway leading to the *Grange* complex, casually looking around. He went to the administration building. He was taken to the manager's office and apologised for arriving unannounced.

'I was in the area and thought I should introduce myself as I am a buyer and seller of horses.'

The manager was the owner, a large, pleasant man. He commented that his son ran the company now as he was semi-retired. The owner made him welcome and invited him to tour the facilities. 'Perhaps we can do business sometime. We don't ever have enough horses to cater for the demand. The northern counties have plenty of butchers, including our own shops, but not enough meat. It's because of this bloody war.'

The administration building had several rooms with five staff.

'We supply the entire northern counties, and the orders and invoices are all sent from here. It's our nerve centre,' the manager said.

Next, he showed him the holding paddocks. 'We don't keep the horses for long. That large building over there is the slaughterhouse and this one just here is where we clean and cure the skins.'

The acting sergeant walked over to where some skins were laid out and he noticed some had the left shoulder section missing – the area where the brand would have been.

He managed to contain his excitement at seeing this vital piece of evidence. After the tour, the manager agreed to meet him again.

When the acting sergeant debriefed them. The small team cheered. They finally had a positive lead. Now all they needed was to catch them in the act. The five of them sat at a table and started throwing ideas around. They agreed that the most logical way to transport stolen horses would be to bring them in with a mob of other horses, legitimately purchased. The team would concentrate on a plan to get access to the rail cars bringing the horses to the *Grange* siding. If this was not possible, they would endeavour to closely look at the horses as they came up the lane to the holding paddock.

Jackson obtained a timetable listing when the freight trains with *Grange* rail cars would arrive at the siding. *Grange* rail cars arrived four days a week. One in the morning and the others in the evening. There was always a crowd around when the freight train arrived.

As other businesses had goods being off-loaded at the same time, Jackson and his team planned to stand around at the siding as disinterested locals, nonchalantly leaning on fences. The acting sergeant would be there in his buyer role. Each of the team knew to look for the arrow brand on the horses as they were being off-loaded.

The person in charge of the off-loading was the owner's son. He even looked like him but without his pleasantness. He was loud and overbearing.

When the buyer introduced himself, the owner's son replied gruffly, 'I'm busy now. I'll be free in about an hour if you want to wait around.'

The buyer nodded and similarly, as the rest of the team, he moved into a position to better view the mob being driven from the rail van and down to the laneway to the *Grange* holding paddocks. There were a hundred plus horses in the mob being unloaded and they came past them in threes and fours.

When the team each reported they had not seen an arrow brand, Jackson decided to try again in two days.

They employed the same plan as previously. This time they were successful. They spotted three horses with the arrow brand. The next morning, they dressed in their Light Horse uniforms and carried arms. When they arrived at the *Grange*, one trooper went to the holding paddock, another trooper went to the slaughterhouse and the other went to the skins shed.

They were to ensure all activity was to be stopped in these three areas. Jackson and the acting sergeant went to the owner's office where he was seated with his son. He looked at the acting sergeant with a puzzled looked.

Jackson introduced himself as Captain Carlsone of the British Army. 'I have reason to believe you have stolen army horses on your property.'

The owner said, 'You are welcome to search my property. We have no stolen horses here. Come with me and inspect the horses. We had some delivered yesterday.'

The son just sat there and made no comment.

Jackson noted this and began to wonder if the owner's son was involved and not the owner.

The four of them went to the paddocks first and after about an hour, did not find any horses with the arrow brand. They then went to the slaughterhouse, where they found twenty-five horses had been slaughtered last night. This would be questioned why later.

They then went to the skinning shed and immediately found twenty-five skins with the Army arrow brand on them. They had not yet been cut off. The owner was shocked. The son still said nothing to support his father.

Captain Carlsone advised them both that he and his troopers were special constables, and they had the power to arrest both of them. They each showed their authority form. Both the owner and the son were arrested and taken to Harrowsgate police station where the police inspector rang Colonel Wood who confirmed the team's authority.

After their reports were written and the evidence handed over to the local police, they went to the Harrowsgate Pub to have a well-earned ale or two.

The following morning, Jackson and his team had an informal meeting with Colonel Lane and his aide. He told the colonel the real reason they had come to his base and the secrecy involved. He also handed him his report on his base. It was complimentary which pleased the new base commander.

The team left Harrowsgate the next day to report to Colonel Woods for their next orders. The debriefing was carried out when Major Walsh and Captain Main, the two officers from the War Department, arrived.

Jackson advised his success was a team effort. He told them, 'We had trouble finding a starting point initially, until we spotted a horse with an Army arrow brand tied to a *Grange* cart. Then we knew where to start. We believed it would require an organisation to be involved in supply and distribution to butchers and eateries in the north.

'When we realised how big the *Grange* organisation was and together with its access to a railway siding, and the number of customers they had, we decided to concentrate on them. The report gives you the details of our planning, investigation and the ultimate result.

'I have heard since it was the son who organised the thefts and managed the stolen Army horses, mixing them with his legally purchased hundred plus. The son of the owner was gaoled, and the company fined. Some of the staff have since been arrested and gaoled for aiding and abetting the thefts. The actual horse thieves have not been identified as yet!'

The major interrupted. 'You and your team have confirmed what a few of us thought but you have proved it, and I must say in a very short period. We have been considering that all railway sidings be manned by the Home Guard.

'If the Home Guard personnel are familiar with horses, perhaps they can carry out ad hoc inspections of the horses disembarking. Hopefully, we can stop, or at least, contain these thefts.

'There are over twenty such sidings in the north counties alone, so can you imagine the number of horses we have lost all over England. We do not have a complete figure. I shall ensure you and your team's records are suitable endorsed with your performance, Well done and goodbye.' They saluted and left, leaving Jackson with the colonel.

The colonel said, 'I will meet you tomorrow after the parade to discuss your next posting. I believe there is a communique due then.'

They had no idea where their next destination might be. The next morning Captain Carlsone went to the colonel's office and was surprised to see Captain Lane in attendance.

He handed sealed orders to Jackson smiling. 'Here's your lucky dip.'

With some apprehension Jackson opened the envelope. After a quick read, he turned to the others. 'We're off to France next week with a consignment of horses. It doesn't surprise me. I am taking horses from here, colonel.'

The colonel replied, 'Yes, I was informed in the same mail. I am to have three hundred horses ready for you within the week. You will leave with them by train to Hull and sail with them to Calais and deliver them to the brigade headquarters. As your orders no doubt state the same.'

Jackson nodded and turned to Captain Lane. 'I'm curious. What is your role here?'

The captain replied, 'I coordinate horse movements throughout England, including the manpower to move them.' He paused. 'I move thousands of horses each year and I need competent teams droving them. I was advised of your team's accomplishments and expertise, so here you are. It's as simple as that. Even though you are Light Horsemen, you are currently unattached.'

Jackson nodded and asked the colonel, 'My men and I will need to be fully winter clothed. Could we select a horse each from your stock?'

The colonel nodded and called his aide, telling him of Jackson's request.

Lieutenant Jackson and his team visited the victualling store and each collected uniforms suitable for cold climates, and a saddle, bridle etc. They already had guns, complete with bayonets and ammunition, plus other items such as a haversack, sleeping blanket, water bottle, saddle bags etc. Afterwards they went to select their horses. The base troopers helped them.

Thirty horses were in a holding yard waiting to be reshoed. They were all good quality horses, so it wasn't difficult to select their horses. They were saddled and ridden by their new owners, who found them acceptable.

They would keep their Light Horse uniforms even with their winter kit for the time being, but in France, they would be required to wear a steel helmet in lieu of their slouch hat with emu feathers.

That night they had a meal at a local café. An annoying old lady kept asking questions about Australia.

Finally, she asked, 'Where did emu feathers come from?'

A trooper answered, 'Well actually, they're kangaroo feathers and they come from here,' and he pointed to his buttocks.

The old lady replied, shaking her head, 'Lucky they live in Australia where it's sunny. They would have cold bums if they lived in England.' Then she wandered off.

CHAPTER TEN

France and Belgium

Departure day arrived with typical English weather – drizzling rain and cold biting wind, the same weather that was causing all the extreme conditions for the soldiers in France and Belgium.

The horses were easily controlled all the way to the railway siding. Colonel Woods had supplied some of his soldiers to assist. The train trip to Hull took most of the day. The horses were expected and were immediately embarked on board the ship.

Each of the team had a bunk, but sleep didn't come easily. The ship was a converted old barge, large but lacking comforts. It had been converted to carry general freight which included livestock. It rolled and pitched continuously during the three-hour voyage.

They arrived early in the morning but had to wait for a vacant wharf space before unloading.

Jackson sent his troopers to check how the horses were handling the pitching and rolling.

The horses were packed into stalls with minimal space. The troopers reported back advising the horses all appeared uninjured.

Several soldiers were seasick while waiting to berth.

After the horses were disembarked, they found three needed to be put down. They had fallen over and been trampled on, quite badly, by the other horses. The loss of three horses out of three hundred horses was acceptable.

When the ship docked, Major James came aboard. He introduced himself as the officer responsible for co-ordinating the supply of horses to the various brigade regimes throughout France and Belgium.

He advised, 'The battles are not going well. We have an immediate need for these horses to be taken to the field ambulances at the Belgium front. I believe your team is very experienced in the care and handling of horses.'

Jackson nodded.

Major James continued. 'You will be briefed on your assignment at the 2nd Field Ambulance station by Captain Jones. Unfortunately, you will be required to wear steel helmets.'

Jackson replied, 'Yes, we are aware of that, but we will keep our emu feathers for later on. When do we move north?'

The major answered, 'Tomorrow at dawn. Regardless of the weather forecast, you go! I'll give you your maps and written directions then. You have plenty of manpower to help droving the herd. There are hundreds and hundreds of soldiers heading to the Front. I suggest you get a good night's sleep. It may be your last for quite some time.'

Dawn came with the forecast of wind and rain.

Jackson sat with the team as Major James explained the directions, using a map laid out on a large table.

'You are to use major roads whenever possible. The trip is estimated to take three to four days. As I said yesterday, you will have a support group of soldiers to assist you. Some of them have travelled this route before. Some fodder is available en route. You will hand over the horses to Captain Jones and give him any assistance you deem fit. We are losing too many horses. You may be there for a month or two. Any questions?'

Jackson replied, 'No. Just let's get the show on the road.'

The horse holding paddock was a hive of activity. The horses had been fed and watered. At the stroke of 0700 hours from the local church bell, the mob of horses started moving out.

The troopers soon had them moving along at a steady pace. They continued for five hours before stopping at a small town's creek where the horses were watered. The rain and wind had not abated and made the country main road slippery. Several horses had nearly lost their footing.

After watering, they moved the mob on for another four hours as daylight was fading. This was their night stop and feed time.

Apart from the weather, the droving had been easy; the horses had stayed together.

The next two days were uneventful. They passed through villages almost destroyed by war. The inhabitants who remained looked as forlorn as did their stray dogs.

The countryside had no cattle grazing, not that there was food for them anyway. The fields were barren with mud and pools of water everywhere. Very few trees were still standing. Destroyed buildings littered the countryside. It was like a scene out of a horror story.

As they neared their destination, the sky was smoky and continuous explosions could be heard ahead of them.

One of Major James' soldiers rode up and advised, 'In an hour we will be close to the Front. I thought you should know, sir.'

Jackson said, 'Thank you. Would you advise my team?'

He nodded and rode off. The wind was carrying the smoke and smell towards them as the noise increased.

The horses were becoming a little agitated, throwing their heads around. Jackson decided to tighten the group. Fortunately, the holding paddock was only ten minutes away. It was a very relieved Jackson, when the gate was closed behind the last of the horses. He thanked Major James' soldiers for their help and released them to be on their way to their barracks.

A horseman rode up and waved. 'Sorry I wasn't here to help. With the way the weather is, I didn't expect you until tomorrow. I'm Captain Jones. Welcome to the Front. How was the trip?'

Jackson smiled. 'I am Captain Carlsone. The trip went quite well. We have nearly three hundred fit horses for you. But we could do with a sleep.'

Captain Jones replied, 'I can give plenty of food and water. Sleep is difficult with the noise of the bombardments. I'll show you the quarters for you and your team and we will meet tomorrow in your tent for a briefing of our situation here.'

That night Jackson began to realise what war was about. The heavy gun salvos with the rifle and the machine gun cracks were continuous. Sometimes there was a muffled boom, possibly a mortar shell or a grenade exploding. As expected, the team had little sleep.

Five bleary eyed soldiers attended the briefing with Captain Jones.

He started. 'As you know we use hundreds and hundreds of horses, mules, donkeys and even a few oxen to tow ambulances, supplies, artillery and ammunition wagons. Headquarters are concerned at the rate of horse losses we're having. Some regiments are losing considerably more than others.'

Captain Jones pointed into the distance. 'For example, there are several field ambulance corps spread out over a hundred miles. As you know thousands of horses are being used close to the Front and consequently many are killed or mortally wounded. Others die because of the bleak weather conditions. We have only a few vets and very few Horsemen. Our wagon drivers have limited horse knowledge.

'Your confidential role will be to record the methods the various regiments use. In particular, the management of their horses and other livestock. You are to make recommendations, as and if, you deem necessary. The reason for your visit is to see if particular regiments have sufficient animals or not. You are to make up your mind and give us realistic figures as you see the situation. Your figures may not necessarily agree with our figures.'

He paused. 'I am aware of your team's performance, particularly your sergeant and your troopers' individual skills – no doubt due to working close to you for well over a year.'

Jackson laughed. 'Yes. We're a close group, and they're good listeners.'

Captain Jones continued. 'As from tomorrow, you will have free reign to move about the battle zones. I suggest you make contact with the senior officer in the zones you visit, for your safety. Head northwest for a start. Here is a letter of authority for each of you. Don't lose it. In some areas you will be given a password. Do not forget it or you may be shot. Well, that's all from me. Any questions?'

Jackson looked around at his team. They shook their heads.

'No, we'll start out tomorrow and send you a weekly report.' The meeting was over. Short and sweet.

The weather was unpredictable, a little sunlight but mostly cloudy and drizzly. They rode out in line, with Captain Carlsone leading and the sergeant bringing up the rear. They could see the value of the horse. They were being used wherever possible. Towing ambulances, gun carriages and supply wagons were standard practice for the horses.

Soldiers were everywhere. Some were fit and marching and some were walking wounded and in bad shape.

As wagons passed, the team would take a quick look at the condition of the horse or horses. They all appeared to be under-weight but generally healthy. The terrain the horses covered could never be handled by a motorised vehicle. There was mud and slush everywhere.

They stopped at a sign saying 'Headquarters'. It was outside a crudely made two room building.

Sandbags were on the roof and the walls had been made from scrap wood, boxes and old canvas.

Captain Carlsone entered and walked over to an officer. He was a colonel seated at a roughly made desk.

He looked up as he was saluted.

'Good afternoon, sir. I am Captain Carlsone.'

The colonel stood and shook his hand. 'Welcome. I have heard of you and your exploits. There are no secrets here.'

Jackson replied, 'Basically, I'm on a fact-finding mission from headquarters to find out if the regiments are satisfied with their livestock levels. As you are no doubt aware the supply line is having trouble keeping up with the demand.'

The colonel nodded. 'I'm happy with my quota. However, seeing you're here, I would like you to give the ones in the paddock the once over. The others are all over the place.'

Jackson nodded. 'Certainly, sir. We can start now.'

The colonel walked to the doorway and pointed.

Jackson could see around a hundred horses in the distance. He saluted the colonel, mounted his horse and signalled his team to follow him.

The inspection revealed no sickness or injuries. The horses were all healthy but a little underweight.

Jackson rode back to report to the colonel, who was pleased with the result.

Jackson asked, 'What do you feed your livestock?'

The answer was, 'Whatever my soldiers can scrounge. When we're in trouble we use sawdust cakes. Believe it or not, it seems to work.'

'Thank you, sir. I know you're busy. We'll be on our way. Goodbye.'

The battles were not going well for the Allies. The death toll and injuries were horrendous. The injured were first taken by stretcher to the regimental aid post which was only two to three hundred yards from the

Front. They were then taken to the advanced dressing station and, if necessary, they were then taken to the field ambulance base. The decision was made here as to the seriousness of the wound or illness.

The soldiers to be sent back to England were then taken by a horse-drawn ambulance to the casualty clearing station which was a mile from the Front. This was occurring all along the Front for miles and miles.

The battalions were at low strength. The casualty lists, now in the thousands, were staggering. The soldiers still in the Front were fighting in terrible conditions – freezing weather with mud everywhere. Some had no food and very little, if any, shelter. Remarkably they could still fight.

German guns were continually landing shells in the Allies area and often some shells were from the Allies whose guns had been accidently fired low, landing short.

There was growing dissent within the Australian senior officers ranks. Some British officers controlling battle orders had never been to the Front. Major losses were occurring because of their total gross incompetence and ignorance of the actual battle situation.

Fortunately, it came to pass, that eventually Australian officers were able to command Australian soldiers.

Jackson was surprised when he heard of this. He had assumed that Australian officers liaised with the British officers and fought alongside each other. But being controlled by British officers? He could understand the Australian's High Command disquiet.

* * *

Suddenly there was a whistling sound, quickly followed by a small explosion. The unusual noise was definitely from a machine, but they had not heard this sound before. They looked up to see an aeroplane with black crosses under its wings. This was the first time they had experienced aerial bombing. Fortunately, no damage was done. The bomb landed in a large mud heap and sprayed mud everywhere. It was only a small bomb, with an air vent which makes a whistling sound when thrown down by the pilot. They watched as the frail two-winged aeroplane turned around, heading back over to German territory with several rifles shooting at it. They were told later these attacks were unpredictable and did little damage.

Some of these aeroplanes took photographs of Allied trench positions and troop movements. This was a major concern. A week later they saw an aeroplane dog fight between three German aeroplanes and two British aeroplanes. The aeroplanes ducked and dived at each other, firing their machine guns, The aerial battle lasted about ten minutes. The Germans damaged an Allied aeroplane, and it was forced to crash land. The pilot escaped injury.

They watched as the other British aeroplane was chased and fired at a German aeroplane which had smoke pouring from its engine. It then spun out of control and exploded when it hit the ground. The remaining aeroplanes called it a day and abandoned the aerial duel.

Jackson and his team were heading in the direction of where the British aeroplane had crash landed. When they arrived, the aeroplane had an armed guard stationed there to stop any pilferers from souveniring parts of the aeroplane.

Although they were not allowed to get close to the aeroplane, they could see it had been badly damaged when trying to land. The wheels had broken from the fuselage, the propellor was shattered, and the two wings and the fuselage badly twisted. They were surprised to see the aeroplane was mainly made of material, wooden struts and connecting wires.

A voice behind them commented, 'I presume by your uniforms you are Australian Light Horse?'

Jackson turned round to see a person dressed in an unusual one piece uniform. He replied, 'Yes. We haven't seen an aeroplane before and as we were passing, we thought we could steal a look. I hope we're not trespassing?'

'No, I'm an Australian from Melbourne. I'm also the pilot who made this mess when trying to land in the paddock. Is there anything you would like to know?' He spent the next half hour answering their questions.

Time to go. They thanked him for his time and his informative presentation. A quick wave, then they rode onto their next ambulance station.

They later found out the pilot was a famous air ace, who had shot down twelve German aeroplanes.

The next field ambulance station was servicing one of the most devastating battles of all. The death toll was in the many thousands and the injuries toll even higher. The station was overflowing.

Jackson volunteered his team to assist wherever they were needed.

A medical orderly said, 'Our greatest need is in the Frontline first aid post, only a few hundred yards from the trenches.'

They were told to report to Doctor Stephenson. They left their horses and walked down to the first aid post.

The noise, smoke and smell became stronger the closer they came. A handmade sign advised them they had arrived.

A harassed officer saw them and asked, 'Are you the volunteers?'

'Yes, we are.'

'Right, I want your lot to separate the walking wounded from those who need immediate attention.'

He pointed. 'The walking wounded are unnecessarily holding up treatment for the seriously wounded. Generally, limb wounds can be stitched and or cleaned then dressed with a bandage and sent on their way. You said you're a vet. You can stitch a wound. Alright, go to it.'

They soon managed to fit in and make an impression.

It was noticeable after a few hours that many wounds requiring attention could be done at the first aid post. The doctor was correct. The injured soldiers outside the station had been reduced to a manageable level. Many wounds had been caused by bullets or shrapnel to soft tissue areas. They required first aid but many were not urgent. Jackson's team attended to them.

Trench foot was of serious concern, but it depended on the extent of the skin damage. The rain made the trenches a quagmire. The duckboards were mainly underwater, but they gave the troops something solid to walk on.

When a soldier's feet were wet day after day in extreme weather, it would lead to gangrene or even amputation. Jackson and his team referred several of these cases to the doctor.

Jackson and the sergeant worked together stitching more than a few soldiers. They were pleased with their handiwork. They wondered what they would think or say if they knew a vet had stitched their wound during the war. Jackson and his team stayed with the first aid post for two weeks and then headed further north.

En route they saw several army brigades and regiments being readied for combat. They camped overnight near them. Next morning, they watched as the troops were assembled, marched out and then arranged into formations. Jackson and his team watched the impressive sight.

A bugle sounded. Thousands of troops were now walking across the countryside into battle in groups. They were heading towards a river. Gunfire erupted from the opposite bank, and this was answered by Allied artillery guns. The artillery fire was accurate and found their targets. The troops were still being hit by machine gun bullets, but they kept advancing until they found areas where they could dig fox holes with their bayonets.

The next day the Allies found the Germans had pulled back. The Allied troops crossed the river unmolested. It had been a costly advance. Many thousands of Australians were killed and wounded. An Australian general was highly critical of the British High Command sending troops in groups and telling them to walk not run, when they were faced with multiple machine gun fire. The troops should have been able to use their initiative.

Jackson and his team were dumbfounded. The carnage was sickening and almost unbelievable.

Why did the troops just keep walking when others alongside them were being slaughtered by machine gun bullets? This was madness. Who was responsible for this mayhem? Some British general playing toy soldiers?

Jackson and his team continued their inspections for nearly three months. A few times they were in danger zones and came under machine gun fire. Often, they stitched up horses' cuts, cleaned wounds and humanely shot a badly injured animal.

Jackson continued to send reports as to why some horses survived better than others. It came down to two issues only.

First, the severe cold weather many malnourished horses had to endure and, second, if they had been in an area where gas had been released, they died much sooner with lung problems.

There were no different issues with the feed and water situation. It was the same everywhere. Water was available but good fodder not available. However, Jackson believed there were adequate numbers of horses available at this time.

The team had become hardened after seeing unbelievable sights and so much carnage. The countryside was barren and had shell craters as far as the eye could see. Villages and farms were destroyed. Dead tree trunks dotted the horizon. They saw valiant but fatal attacks over open ground with the soldiers being slaughtered. Barb wire also caused havoc during the attacks.

The noise from the continuous machine gun fire and hand grenades exploding was deafening and nerve-racking, not forgetting the mud, slush and puddles the soldiers endured plus lice and serious stomach upsets. The soldiers' living conditions were atrocious. It was a shambles of the worst order.

CHAPTER ELEVEN

Germans Captured

Captain Jones had forwarded new orders. The team were to return to Egypt to join a new desert mounted brigade. They were delighted to be attached to the Light Horse again. They started to prepare for their return journey.

A few days later, Jackson was looking at an ammunition wagon being towed by two horses. The offside horse was dragging its rear hind leg, so he signalled the driver to let him ride with him. He sat behind the horse and his suspicion was confirmed. The horse had arthritis and would be in some pain. He should be retired. He couldn't be cured.

The driver and Jackson chatted until he asked, 'Where is the Front?'

The driver pointed to a small rise in the road. 'It's four hundred yards on the other side of that hill, and we're being pushed back.'

As the driver started to turn the horses away from the direction of the Front, they suddenly saw a group of Germans only ten yards away. Their machine gun was facing away from them, in the direction of the Allied trenches. Jackson drew his revolver as the driver grabbed his rifle.

The Germans were as surprised they were. They had not heard them approaching due to the battle noise from the Front. A German fired a pistol at them and hit one of the horses. Jackson fired and shot him in the shoulder. He then fired from point blank range at two others, killing them instantly. The driver covered the other two with his rifle and watched the German who shot the horse get a belting,

Jackson had holstered his revolver and had begun punching the German soldier and he kept hitting him, yelling, 'I'll teach you to shoot a horse, you mongrel.'

The driver thought, *I wouldn't want to upset him.*

Finally, the German collapsed. Jackson cooled down and after the other two Germans' hands were tied, they sat on the ammunition boxes together with the captured machine gun and their ammunition. The bullet had struck the horse in the rump. Jackson later removed the bullet without difficulty. The horse was not duly affected.

The local colonel praised the two of them for their efforts. However, the driver was censured for getting that close to the enemy with a wagon loaded with ammunition and firearms.

The colonel admitted that they were unaware the Germans had infiltrated that zone. Finding them before they could cause any damage had alerted the Allied Forward Command Post.

* * *

Next day, as the team was preparing to depart for Calais, a bomb exploded close to Jackson and a large piece of shrapnel struck him in his right leg. He sustained a large two inch deep cut to his rear upper leg muscle almost severing the muscle. The field ambulance base doctor cleaned the wound, stitched the two ends together and then tightly bound the wound. It was painful but bearable.

He was told he was off to England for a surgeon to operate on the damaged muscle. He was more disappointed about not being able to go to Egypt with his team, than worried about his injury. After the team said their farewells and promised to keep in contact they went their separate ways, to Egypt and England.

CHAPTER TWELVE

A Dangerous Liaison

Michael poured himself a cup of tea then went out to his porch to sit and sort his mail. The first letter he opened was from Jackson. In some ways he was envious of him and his military life, taking him to different countries. Although all letters were censored, the newspapers gave him an idea where he might be.

Michael felt his saddlery business life was boring. He would be doing the same thing until the day he died. He craved to be doing something exciting. He sat back and thought about what had happened in the last year.

Late in 1916, Michael's father mortgaged the Riverbank property to purchase a business premises in Melbourne and Michael had offered to take over the mortgage repayments from the profits of the Riverbank business. His mother and father moved to Melbourne and left him to show his business capability. They agreed that his father would mainly manufacture rugs, furniture seats and backs, coats, carry bags and wagon seats. Michael would mainly manufacture saddles, bridles, belts and gun holsters.

Michael found the going tough working with only a young helper, but he had managed to keep up with the mortgage repayments and had shown a small profit.

Six months later, a crewman from a riverboat came in and asked him if he wanted to buy some skins. Quality skins were always in demand.

Michael said. 'Yes, where are they?'

The crewman answered, 'On my boat at the north end of the pier.'

Michael replied, 'I'll be there at five p.m.'

The crewman nodded and left.

At five p.m. Michael was at the pier. The crewman was waiting and waved to him. When he boarded the riverboat, he was introduced to the captain-owner, Willy Mays. He was short and stocky with a mean piercing look. Michael was immediately cautious.

They took Michael below to see the skins. They were good quality. They had twenty cow skins, and the price was reasonable. Michael purchased them. The next day he sent his young helper along to collect them. He sent ten of them to his father who was delighted with the quality.

He commented, 'These must have come from a prime herd.'

Michael then realised that he had not asked where the skins came from. He went to his helper and asked, 'What brands were on the skins?'

The helper replied, 'None. They had been cut out.'

Two weeks later Michael had a serious accident and broke his leg. Eventually the crewman returned and offered more skins. Michael commented on the lack of brands on the skins.

'You should have known that when you purchased the first lot. You're implicated now,' the crewman answered.

Michael knew any whisper of livestock theft in the bush was a death knell for a business. They had him over a barrel.

A month later Michael was still hobbling around with his broken leg, using a crutch and with a rapidly dwindling bank balance. He had not been able to work for three weeks.

When he was approached to accept more cowskins on credit, he said, 'Yes, I have no choice! But I want the hides cut into the largest rectangle possible, no legs or sides. Agreed?'

The crewman nodded and walked off.

When Michael received his first shipment of ten hides, he went to work immediately. He used the templates for his various leather products and marked the rectangular hide with their shapes. He worked through the night cutting out the hide shapes to be stitched together. Within four hours the hides were no more, with very little wastage. If the police came, he could plead ignorance of the shoulder brands.

That night Michael wondered where they were getting the cow hides. The riverboats travelled hundreds of miles along the Murray River, where there were some dairy herds. Was this a coincidence or not? He continued accepting a few hides and getting himself deeper in debt.

Michael and Jane had continued seeing each other at the Saturday dance. They began to grow closer with both Jackson and Mary away from Riverbank, serving overseas. Recklessly, they continued their relationship. Michael began spending more time at her farm, supposedly doing odd jobs. Her father had died, and her mother was confined to a wheelchair at the farm.

It got to the stage where he would stay overnight in a spare bedroom. Although they had not slept together, the writing was on the wall. Jane was still a virgin and for all intents and purposes, she intended saving herself for Jackson. Alcohol and loneliness were her downfall. Normally, she imbibed very little. A sherry or two was her limit.

Her birthday was a quiet dinner at the farm with only the two of them. Her mother always dined early and then went to bed. During dinner, Jane had two wines which made her feel very mellow.

After dining, Michael put a record on the gramophone. It was a slow waltz.

Jane had another wine and another. She threw discretion to the wind when Michael kissed her and returned the kiss with the passion of a lonely young woman.

Eventually, without thinking, she allowed Michael to lead her to the bedroom. They lay on the bed kissing. Michael took the initiative and began to undo her top. Soon they were both naked on the bed and kissing passionately. Michael slowly entered her, and her legs wrapped around him.

Jane mumbled something he didn't understand.

When it was over, Jane remained motionless and speechless, realising what had happened. She didn't answer Michael's questions, so he pulled a blanket over her and sat watching her until she went to sleep. He slept in a spare room.

The next morning was difficult for them. They both felt guilty, particularly Michael. It was her first time, but it had not been his first experience.

Jane did not blame him. She felt she was at fault.

They had a quiet breakfast together, with very little conversation. There would be time for that later. They parted, Michael went to town and Jane saddled a horse and went for a ride to clear her head and think of the ramifications of what had happened.

Michael returned the following week to see how Jane was feeling. She greeted him and invited him in for tea.

Jane started talking. 'I don't blame you for what happened. I'm finding loneliness difficult to handle. I've had feelings before but have managed to keep them under control. Perhaps the wines released my inhibitions. It's happened, so be it.'

Michael took her hand. 'You won't be lonely anymore.'

Jane replied, 'Yes, I have feelings for you. We can continue to see each other and see what the future brings.' Neither of them mentioned who was on both of their minds – Jackson! They were ignoring the inevitable, for now.

Apart from Jane, Michael had become a loner and began to spend time at the wharves with the riverboat men. They were a rough lot, enjoying drinking and gambling, and often invited him to join them. Eventually he wavered and began to spend more time with them. He started gambling and was successful for a while and he was able to pay back his debt to Captain Mays.

CHAPTER THIRTEEN

The Investigation

Michael was surprised to see the local police sergeant enter the shop.

'Morning, sergeant. This is a surprise. What's happening?'

The sergeant said, 'G'day. It's just a routine call. There's been some livestock stealing along the Murray River stations. If you hear anything, let me know.'

Michael said, 'Of course I will, but I've heard nothing like that.'

The sergeant nodded and left the shop.

A week later the sergeant was back with a constable. He said, 'I hope you don't mind but I would like to examine your hides. It's just a routine check. You're the fourth business we've checked.'

Michael replied, 'Certainly, free to search anywhere you wish.'

After a fruitless search, the sergeant returned. 'Thank you, Michael, for your patience. All's good. Bye for now.'

* * *

Finally, Michael stood up to the captain. 'The local police have visited me twice in the last fortnight and inspected my stock of hides and they mentioned they thought riverboats were involved in moving cattle. I suggest you stay clean for a while. They said they had seen me at the wharf several times and that's why they inspected my stock.'

Captain Mays walked away saying. 'We'll meet again.'

Michael returned to reading the local newspaper and was interested in an article about the loss of valuable livestock along the Murray River and that a police investigation was to be carried out by Chief Inspector Miles Gemini from Ballarat.

Michael would need to be extra cautious in his dealings with Captain Mays, now a top cop was involved.

He had just had dealings with the captain. A short time ago, he had just walked in out of the blue to Michael's workshop and said, 'I need your expertise. I've been to an auction and obtained a consignment of saddles. I know nothing of the marketing of saddles. You know the buyers and you can retain thirty-five per cent of the selling price.'

Michael asked, 'Show me an auction invoice before I agree to sell them.'

Captain Mays pulled a crumpled piece of paper from his pocket and handed it to Michael. 'What type of saddles are they?'

'I believe they are what you would call stockman saddles.'

'Do you have one with you?'

The captain walked to the doorway and waved. One of his crew carried a saddle into the workshop and placed it on a bench.

Michael could see it was good quality and a valuable saddle.

The captain said, 'I have nine more identical to this one and all in perfect condition.'

Michael looked at him and said, 'Well it will be good to do legal business with you for a change. Yes, I'll sell them. The larger stables in Melbourne always have buyers for good saddles.'

Michael took a train to Melbourne with a sample saddle. He borrowed a horse from his father and visited several stables. He sold the ten within the day. When he returned to Riverbank, he freighted the sold saddles to the respective stables as agreed.

A week later Captain Mays appeared on his doorstep. Michael paid him his money less his thirty-five per cent. He asked him if he could get some more from auctions.

The captain replied, 'I doubt it, but I'll keep my ears and eyes open.'

Michael was becoming nervous with a police chief inspector investigating in the district.

Two weeks later, an out-of-towner wandered into Michael's workshop and introduced himself as an insurance inspector. He told him of a train derailment the month before over the border in New South Wales, where the guardsman was injured. The train driver and the stoker had carried him several miles to a doctor. When the driver and the stoker returned, the train had been robbed. Freight stolen consisted of saddles, fifty of them. Also, some guns were missing, presumed stolen.

'I'm travelling around asking people in the industry, like yourself, if any saddles have been offered to you.'

Michael shook his head. 'No, this is only a small town. I'd imagine they would try to sell them in Sydney. You'd never be able to trace the culprits there.'

The insurance inspector agreed. 'You're probably right. Goodbye.'

Michael began to wonder just how authentic the invoice was that the captain had shown him. He had trapped him again to be involved in another shady deal. In one way the extra money had helped Michael's mortgage repayments. But at what future cost?

Two weeks later Michael opened his weekly newspaper. He was confronted by a full-page photograph of Jackson and Mary at the presentation of his Military Cross by King George V to Captain Carlsone, who had been badly wounded in France. The article then quoted the words on the citation.

Riverbank now had a homegrown hero. He was the talk of the town. Mary was not forgotten. Her service in Gallipoli and in England was mentioned as well and how the two of them had met in England during Michael's months of rehabilitation in hospital after being wounded in action.

When Jane saw the photograph in the newspaper, she suffered an enormous bout of guilt. She wondered where she was heading and how she could stop this relationship. She would go for long walks with her dogs along the riverbank. How and why had she allowed this situation to occur and get out of hand?

She shook her head. 'Fool, fool, that I am!' Jackson would return one day. She was fearful what the outcome would be if he found out about her indiscretion. Particularly as she had seen how violent his rage could be.

With difficulty, she answered Jackson's letters but found it hard to be affectionate in her replies, as her guilt complex took over.

She enjoyed being with Michael and he was devoted to her. She knew it was wrong but what should she do? How could she tell Michael the guilt she felt?

When she broached the subject with Michael, he angrily replied, 'I'll let Jackson know you are having an affair.' He was bluffing but this comment made her realise she was in an impossible no-win position. She became resigned to her fate.

The newspaper also had a story of an Australian Light Horse victory in Palestine.

It described how hundreds of Australian Light Horsemen charged and defeated a well-defended Turkish position. Little did Jane consider Jackson had been one of those Light Horsemen and he had been wounded for a second time.

Michael and Jane were beginning to argue about trivial issues. The pressure on their sordid relationship was beginning to tell, although they both allowed it to continue.

When the photo and the story became common knowledge, they found that they were often ignored. Some people wouldn't even talk to them. People who had ignored their liaison before, now spoke openly about it. It was now an open scandal.

One night a few drunks saw Michael walking home and began shouting. 'Wait until Jackson comes home. You'll be for it. He'll thrash you, good and proper, you bastard.'

Michael knew they were right.

Another drunk saw him and came over. 'I wouldn't piss on you if were on fire.' He walked away, then came back. 'On second thoughts. I would piss on you, you prick.'

Michael began thinking of leaving town to live in Melbourne. His business takings began to decline, and he was having problems keeping up with his bank payments. His bank overdraft had reached its limit and Jane stopped loaning him money. However, she did pay him for the work he did on her farm.

Michael began drinking more with his friends on the docks and gambling with money he just didn't have. To repay his debt, he was forced by Captain Mays to sell some of the suspect skins to other saddlers and leather merchants.

CHAPTER FOURTEEN

Now the Police

Inspector Miles Gemini had been a member of the Victorian Police force for twenty-three years. He was a farm boy, reared on a farm in central Victoria.

Born in 1880 when Victoria was part of the Colony of New South Wales, he had risen quickly up through the ranks, and he was now the chief inspector in charge of the Northern District of Victoria. He was well known for his success in solving major crime investigations. The criminal world knew his reputation and were wary whenever his name was mentioned.

The chief considered Michael to be of no major interest at the moment even though his sales of skins to other merchants had come to the notice of the chief inspector's team.

He was just a pawn in this matter. He would get to him later. He and his team would concentrate on the riverboats' connection first.

Livestock theft of valuable rams, ewes, lambs and, surprisingly, cows had been a concern for the landowners with river boundaries for over a year. The river was over fifteen hundred miles long, but the police were concentrating on an area of a few hundred miles towards the South Australian border. This was the area where almost all thefts were occurring, The Victorian police were turning their attention to the commercial riverboats plying on the Murray River.

As the river was in the state of New South Wales, this complicated the Victorian police's pursuit of criminals. The chief inspector was looking for common links to the thefts. The river was the only link so far. He had several questions he was trying to answer, amongst them: How were the livestock being removed from the properties? How were they being transported? Where were they being sold? Who were the ring leaders? Who were the middlemen?

Several undercover police visited the river towns, particularly where the towns had a wharf. It took four weeks before a clue was found. A wharf had been washed down the previous night and no sheep were scheduled to be loaded during that night. Sheep droppings were found on the wharf early the following morning.

Unfortunately, six riverboats had visited the wharf overnight. But at least this narrowed the number of riverboats concerned down to six. Coincidently a local theft had been reported the next day. Twenty merino lambs had gone missing. There were holding pens at the wharf, and they always had sheep in them waiting to be loaded. Their baaing all night would hide the noise of a few lambs being loaded onto a riverboat. A two-horse wagon only would be needed to transport such a small number of lambs.

The next question was: Which direction were the riverboats heading – upstream or downstream?

Remarkably, the police were told by a river lock master that they were all heading downstream to the South Australian border. The police now had some solid information.

Chief Inspector Gemini briefed his team. He pointed to a chart on the wall. 'There are only three more wharfs in Victoria before the South Australian border. If the thieves unload any of their livestock at any of these wharfs, we will catch them, but as they know we're looking for them, I think they'll be taking them to South Australia and will offload them at the first wharf over the border. There is a lock here just before the border and after the last Victorian wharf. I want that lock to be under surveillance twenty-four hours each day. A riverboat will be in the lock for at least ten minutes. Get as close you can to it and look and listen. Do not search or arouse suspicion. If you believe the riverboat should be searched, ring me. I have the support of the South Australian police. They have agreed to search any boat we recommend.'

The team smiled their agreement with the plan.

Three days later the inspector received the call he was waiting for. Lambs had been heard from Captain Mays' riverboat at the last river lock. He rang the South Australian police with the news and the morning after he was advised that they had found nineteen merino lambs in the hold of the riverboat. There were also a number of cow skins on the deck, some with the brand removed. They had arrested the crew. The law unfortunately required Captain Mays and his crew to be charged with theft under South Australian law.

In a plea for clemency, Captain Mays told the story of how he received the cow skins. 'Two brothers erected a slaughterhouse and were purchasing stolen cows and butchering them for the district butcher shops. The merino lambs were being delivered for a friend, who is a broker. He would have sold them on.' He did not admit to any other thefts. The broker was later arrested.

The captain continued, 'When I found out the value of skins from Michael, I trapped him into buying the skins from the stolen cows.' He also admitted, 'I have been involved in the movement of stolen rams, but I haven't seen the contact person, since he knew of your investigation. I don't know his full name or where he's from? He contacts me.'

Inspector Gemini sat down. His job was partly over. But now he had the dilemma of what to do about Michael. He wasn't a major player, but could he be useful in leading him to the middlemen and ultimately to the ring leaders? The thefts had been planned by persons knowing the stations along the Murray River. Perhaps they were riverboat crewmen.

After the arrests, thefts along the Murray River declined dramatically.

Michael failed to realise his life had become a series of potential disasters and that he was spiralling out of control. If he did not change the direction his life was heading in he would soon reach a point of no return. He was virtually friendless, but who could he turn to?

CHAPTER FIFTEEN

Two Meet Again

After Mary had followed Jackson's lead and joined the AIF Nursing Corp, she saw very little of Michael or Jane. She completed two years nursing training at the district hospital as a triage nurse. She was a junior nurse and was still on a learning curve, but nurses had been needed and she was recruited and sent to assist the Australian wounded at Gallipoli. She was now in a rehab hospital in England.

She continued to correspond with both Michael and Jane and looked forward to reading their responses. Michael and Mary had remained friends but there was never a romance on the horizon. Every month or so she received a letter from Jackson. Sometimes their letters overlapped but they were still a pleasure to receive.

Jackson was depressed. He had trouble accepting that he was incapacitated and would remain so for several months. The ship had hundreds of wounded and ill soldiers aboard. They travelled in darkness as submarines were always on the prowl. Boredom was difficult for him to accept. Time dragged on.

After arriving in England, the wounded were dispersed throughout the various county hospitals. Jackson went to a large hospital in Manchester.

The surgeon was an impressive grey-haired man. He introduced himself as Professor William Black. 'You can call me Bill. Let's have a look at your problem. I've read your file. You were lucky it just missed the artery.'

The nurse unbandaged the injury. Bill looked at it and touched the areas around it. 'Do you feel my touch?'

Jackson nodded. 'Yes.'

Bill said, 'Good! There's no nerve damage then. I can repair the damage to your muscle, but it will be a long recuperation. We will operate tomorrow.'

Jackson wrote a letter to Jane telling her of the professor's good news. He hadn't received any mail for over two months and with his last move, he expected further delays to his mail.

The operation went ahead on time and was successful. When he woke up, he saw Bill's smiling face staring down at him. 'Welcome back. The operation was successful. Now you will go to a rehab hospital for around two months and then you should be able to walk. You may have a slight limp, but it won't affect your life's routine.'

Bill sat on the bed. 'I remember being in a hospital talking with an extremely naïve elderly associate of mine, and he commented about the unusual exercises you Australians do. He watched, from a distance, a circle of Australians, who, every thirty seconds or so, would throw up their arms in the air and yell something and then they would all bend down. I didn't have the heart to tell him that it was a gambling game called two-up. Goodbye and good luck.' They shook hands and gave a wave to each other.

The hospital where he had his operation was very busy. Jackson was moved out the next day and driven to a rehab hospital. This hospital was a hive of activity. There were wheelchairs and crutches everywhere. He was wheeled to a bed next to a window overlooking a large open green grass area with seats and colourful flower beds. Just the calm view he needed for relaxation and recuperation.

His therapy consisted of leg movements in bed. A nurse would slowly lift the lower leg at the ankle and gradually stretch the damaged leg muscle ten times per session, increasing the angular movement of the whole leg at the knee.

He was taken for a wheelchair outing every second day. One day he spotted a nurse he thought was Mary Giles. No, it couldn't be! He asked the next nurse he saw if she knew of a nurse called Mary Giles working in this hospital.

She answered, 'No, but there are many nurses here I don't know. I'll ask around for you.'

Two days later he awoke to a voice. 'Hello stranger.' It was Mary Giles smiling down at him. She had tears in her eyes. They hugged each other.

Jackson said, 'God, it's good to see you. I've thought of you often, wondering where you were. I haven't received any mail for over two months.'

Mary said, 'I only found out you were here ten minutes ago. The nurse you spoke to the other day saw my name on my badge and told me you were here. It's good to talk with you. Come on, get up, you're getting a wheelchair trip with me.'

For a change the sun was shining, a pleasant day for an outing. They parked near a bench seat and Mary helped Jackson onto it from the wheelchair.

Jackson commenced talking. 'A lot of water has past under the bridge since early 1915. I've seen enough horror to last me forever and I've seen some beautiful sights. This wound has made me think of life. How has your war treated you?'

Mary looked at him and told him of the Gallipoli hospital ship and the incident where her friend nearly died.

Jackson felt they were kindred spirits. They both felt better after talking about their experiences. They sat in the sun holding hands.

Mary wisely changed the subject. 'I wonder what's happening at Riverbank at this moment.'

Jackson laughed. 'Well, it would be 0500 hours – in the morning. Probably not much.'

Mary smiled. 'You know what I mean. Anyhow the dairy farmers would be up and about.'

They chattered for a while longer and then, as Mary had other duties to attend to, she wheeled Jackson back to his bed.

Two soldiers in the next two beds were laughing. One looked at Jackson. 'I've just heard the best joke yet. You'll like it. The Germans were looking for prisoners with skills. After hearing several soldiers tell of their skills, they came to an Australian who said, "My profession will impress you, and I would prefer to look after twenty German soldiers than one British soldier." The German officer said, "You Australians were raised from convicts. I understand your feelings. What is your profession?" "I'm an undertaker," he answered. Even the German officer walked away laughing.'

Jackson laughed with the other soldiers. Even in war there is humour.

Mary promised to return and see him each day.

As her experience had only been as a triage nurse, it was felt she needed a change to general duties.

The matron walked over and introduced herself. 'How are you being treated, captain. I'm sorry I haven't met you sooner, but the hospital administration takes up most of my time.'

Jackson replied, 'Nurse Giles is from my hometown and drops by to say hello. I'm fine, thanks.'

The matron continued, 'We have a special visitor in two days. You and several others have been named to meet him. I don't know who he is myself. We'll spruce you up, trim your beard and hair, provide you with fresh clothes. Bye for now. I'll see you then.'

Jackson mentioned it to Mary, but she knew nothing, only that a VIP was coming.

From his bedside window, he could see chairs being laid out and a podium being erected on the lawn. Gardeners were busy trimming plants. The area was neat and colourful.

The day arrived with the hospital a hive of activity.

Jackson was given a new set of pyjamas, a dressing gown and slippers. He had progressed to a walking stick, although he always had a nurse with him during his daily walks.

Mary had organised to be with Jackson as his attendant.

A lieutenant approached them. He saluted and asked, 'Good morning. Am I addressing Captain Carlsone?'

Jackson nodded. 'Yes.'

The lieutenant asked, 'Would you and your attendant come with me, sir? I'll escort you to your seats.' The two of them followed him to the front row of seats.

'Thank you, Lieutenant. We will have a good view of the proceedings.'

The officer saluted him, and Jackson sat down. Mary sat in a seat behind him.

The great moment had arrived. They could see a large gathering approaching with generals and suddenly they were amazed to see King George V in their midst coming towards them. The assembly all stood until the King was seated.

A general delivered a welcoming speech and then the King rose and joined the general. He then began to call soldiers forward for decorations and awards.

After three soldiers had their medals pinned on them by the King, Jackson was stunned to hear his name called. With wobbly steps he went forward, stood in front of the King and bowed his head. He then stood upright, listening to the words on the citation. It was for the incident in Belgium, the ammunition, the gunfight killing several enemy soldiers, capturing the German machine gun post and discovering a new German incursion. He was awarded the Military Cross.

The King said, 'Well done. You are a credit to your country.' He then pinned the medal onto his gown.

Jackson replied, 'Thank you, Your Majesty.' He stepped back, bowed and returned to his seat still in a daze.

Mary lent forward and whispered, 'You're now famous in Riverbank.'

After the King left, a photographer took a picture of both Jackson and Mary in their uniforms. Mary had quickly borrowed one for Jackson from another Light Horse patient. The photographer sent one to the local Riverbank newspaper editor.

Jackson said, 'Now we're both famous in Riverbank'.

Jackson was pleasantly surprised at Mary's self-confidence. She was no longer a reserved country girl.

Mary had noticed a similar change in Jackson. He was a natural born leader and he now spoke with commanding authority. She wondered if he would remain with the Light Horse or start a veterinary business. She believed he would be a success whatever direction he decided to follow. She visited him every day and it was obvious they were becoming more than friends.

They both realised this and also that Jackson would eventually be posted to the 4th Light Horse Regiment in Egypt. They kept their feelings for each other to themselves because of Jane.

Mary received news about Michael and Jane's closeness but believed it was not for her to tell Jackson rumours.

Jackson's progress was on target.

His daily leg exercises had the injured right muscle almost stretching the same as the left muscle. He had progressed to slowly walking a few yards.

Lying in bed for so long had left him unfit. He wouldn't be returning to duty until he could satisfy a doctor that he was capable of assuming a command.

Mary enjoyed going to the pictures with him as a self-appointed minder. She happily wheeled him to the theatre. As a recovering wounded soldier, he wore a blue arm band; they often didn't have to pay. They sat arm in arm at the pictures, Mary often resting her head on Jackson's shoulder.

It was three months before Jackson was confirmed fit for service. His orders arrived, informing him to proceed to the nearest port and board the next ship sailing to Egypt. On arrival, he was to report to the officer commanding the 4th Light Horse Regiment.

Mary took the news stoically. They agreed to write often. She wanted to cry but not in front of Jackson. They had grown closer than they had realised.

Jackson wisely decided to make their goodbyes quickly. He said, 'We will meet again.'

She nodded, controlling her tears.

They kissed with a controlled passion. Jackson turned and boarded the vehicle taking him to the station. They waved to each other.

About this time the term 'digger' emerged. It originated from the New Zealanders who were known as gum diggers. The name digger soon included the Australians who enjoyed the term.

Jackson was happy to be called digger in the hospital, even though he was an officer.

CHAPTER SIXTEEN

The Sinai

The ship was full of troops and equipment bound for the Middle East campaign. After leaving the English port they joined a convoy of twenty ships spread out to the horizon. The weather was squally and pitched the ships around, making many soldiers seasick. The weather remained the same until the convoy entered the Mediterranean Sea. The next day the sun was shining and the seas reasonably calm. They sailed nonstop until they arrived in Cairo.

They had two submarine warnings but the destroyers, as usual, frightened them away. Watching these graceful ships speeding through the convoy dropping depth charges and seeing the eventual explosions was exciting and one hoped that they actually sunk a submarine. These incidents helped break the monotony of the voyage.

Captain Carlsone entered the headquarters building and was directed to the office of the Light Horse Commander-in-Chief. He was shown in by an aide. He saluted and was motioned to a chair. There were three other officers in the room.

The brigadier said, 'Your achievements precede you. Congratulations on your MC. I believe you wanted to join the Light Horse and you were posted to the 4th Light Horse Regiment. They will be departing at the end of the month. You will be responsible for overseeing the overall condition of several hundred horses. You will have time to select any support men you consider you may need. You will have a free hand and you only report to me. As a veterinary officer who has seen active service at the Front in both Gallipoli and France, your experience will be invaluable. You will find the horses here are in better condition. As you know the Walers handle the hot sunny weather better than the wet cold weather. It will be quite a change of weather for you. Good luck. There is a sergeant outside, who you know. He will show you around.' Jackson saluted and left the office.

Jackson recognised the voice before he saw him. It was his first sergeant who had taken him under his wing when he had first been given a squad to lead. He returned his salute. 'This is a pleasant surprise. How has the war treated you? We will have plenty to talk about.'

The sergeant smiled. 'Apart from being torpedoed and getting a bullet in my shoulder, I've been lucky. Congratulations on your Military Cross.' He continued, 'I have been instructed to take you to your accommodation. We can talk on the way.'

'I heard you were torpedoed. I would imagine it was quite an ordeal.'

The sergeant looked at Jackson and smiled. 'That's an understatement; it frightened the daylights out of me. I was below deck when the sirens started and a minute or so later, I heard this enormous explosion. It made the ship rock. I immediately headed to a ladder and climbed to the main deck. The ship was down at the bow with smoke pouring from that area. Surprisingly there was no panic. Soldiers were spilling onto the main deck in a reasonably orderly manner. The ships' company were efficient; the gun crews ran to their guns, the fire crews went for'ard as directed and the duty crew were preparing the lifeboats, in case they were needed. The bridge was calling for a damage report. The ship had been in battle readiness. This required all the ships' doors and hatches to be closed immediately after they had been opened for use.

'Even though the ship was down at the bow, it was still underway, slowly but definitely moving forward. The damage to the bow was extensive and the ship was slowly sinking. I grabbed a life vest from a deck locker. Fortunately, we had boat drills two days before. As the ship slowly sank the order was given "Abandon ship". It was definitely sinking. A destroyer had moved close to our ship ready to pick up the soldiers and ship's crew. Our lifeboats were readied to be lowered and we all queued to climb into them. The ship's crew then swung out the davits and lowered the boat into the water. Each boat had two sailors who released the boat free from the ship's davits. One sailor started the engine and the other steered. The sea was turbulent, but I had confidence in the crew.'

He took a deep breath, 'Suddenly the badly damaged ship listed to port, beginning to roll and the scene became chaotic. The few remaining soldiers and sailors were leaping into the sea and swimming away from the ship to escape the water turbulence and vortex created by the sinking ship. All the lifeboats had been launched and were now concentrating on assisting the men in the sea. The men in the sea all had time to put a on life vest, hence no lives were lost. Only the ship.

'As per tradition, the captain was the last sailor to dive from the ship and swim to a lifeboat.

'I watched as the ship began to pitch up and slowly sink beneath the waves. The sea was littered with debris from the ship. In a few minutes it was all that remained. The destroyer collected us and took us to Cairo, and I was given seven days leave, and here I am.'

Jackson replied, 'You should write a book when you get home. You've had a very interesting and exciting time. It's good to see you still in one piece.'

The sergeant continued, 'The Light Horse Regiments have been training for several months in preparation to go into Syria. Headquarters are concerned about the Suez Canal being taken by the Turks and becoming a threat to Egypt. It's of interest to know the Suez Canal is classed as a Neutral Zone and is a Protectorate of Great Britain.'

Jackson nodded and asked, 'Do you know the whereabouts of any of your team?'

The sergeant nodded. 'Yes, three were invalided to Australia after a stint in England. They were in a gas attack. I lost track of the other trooper. I was lucky. I had gone back to the rear with the bullet wound in my shoulder and wasn't there when it happened. The last I saw of them they were in bad shape. They could hardly walk to the ambulance to take them to the train.

I'm glad I was transferred here. That gas is immoral. I wouldn't wish that on my worst enemy.

'What of your team?'

Jackson shook his head. 'I wrote to each of them when I was in rehab, but I am yet to receive an answer from any of them. Although my mail is always unpredictable.'

The sergeant stopped and pointed. 'Your palace awaits you, sir. Commonly called a tent. You'll find them comfortable except when the desert dust storms blow. I understand I'm attached to your team, but I have no written orders.'

Jackson replied, 'I answer only to the brigadier, so I don't think that will be a problem. Meet me here tomorrow around 1000 hours.' They saluted and Jackson entered the tent.

The tent had two bunks and a rig on which clothes could be hung. There were no home comforts.

Another officer walked in and smiled. 'Hello, I'm Henry Butler. I'm new and I've just arrived.'

'I'm Jackson Carlsone and I've just arrived as well.'

Henry said, 'I've heard of you and your Military Cross. Well done. What's your role here?'

'I'm a vet and I'm here to monitor the condition of the horses of the regiment. What's yours?'

Henry said, 'I've just arrived from Australia, and I haven't any idea yet. I'm to meet with the colonel tomorrow and then be told what is expected from me. I understand something important is about to happen. I'm looking forward to some action.'

Jackson looked at him and answered, 'It's not all beer and skittles out there.'

Authority was somewhat ignored by the Australians.

Some would only salute Australian officers. An incident occurred when a group of Light Horsemen were told by their own officers that they must salute the British officers.

A group of Australians were walking down a Cairo Street and along came a British private. A corporal in the Australian group called, 'Eyes right,' and the corporal saluted the private and then ordered, 'Eyes front.' The British private was totally confused and didn't see the funny side of the Australian humour.

A British officer standing on the other side of the road was talking with a French officer and said, 'Did you see that! The Australians have no respect for officers, or discipline.'

The French officer said, 'Ah yes, but they can fight.'

The British officer mused, 'Yes, that's true.'

There was an air of excitement with the preparations to move accelerating. Jackson wanted three more men on his team before they left Egypt. He found them in the casualty ward.

One trooper was on light duties recovering from a broken wrist and the other trooper was recovering from a badly bruised thigh muscle. He could walk but was unable to ride freely. They were both experienced stockmen from cattle stations and more importantly, they knew horses.

The sergeant located one of their former squad and Jackson had him transferred to his team.

Jackson briefed his team. They were to watch how the Light Horsemen were managing their horses. 'We will split up and unobtrusively watch for faults in what they may be doing. You are not to interfere, but to report back to me later in the morning. We have over three hundred horses and we only have a matter of weeks to do this. Any advice you feel a trooper may need, will be advised to them by the sergeant and myself. We start at 0800 hours tomorrow.'

The inspection progress and issues were advised in writing to the brigadier daily. Troopers' names were not recorded. The brigadier had confidence in Captain Carlsone to resolve any problems he identified. He had more important things on his mind.

The inspection proved worthwhile. Generally, the horsemen treated their horses very well. Only a few were not curry combing their horse correctly and a few did not clean their horse's hooves. They willingly accepted the advice given to them by Captain Carlsone and the sergeant. These horsemen were new to the regiment and from the city and hadn't the experience of the bushmen. The regiment's horses were in good condition and fit. They were exercised each day and handled the hot conditions without trouble.

Only a few needed any medical attention. One had a bowel problem. This was fixed with a good warm water enema. Others needed their eyes flushed after a desert storm. Another had a long cut to his rump when he backed into a supply box bound with metal bands. He let the sergeant stitch the cut, as Jackson explained the procedure to the two troopers. 'You may have to do this yourselves one day, when I'm not around.'

The brigadier called a meeting of his officers to brief them on their next campaign. He started, 'Gentlemen, from tomorrow onwards, we are destined to make history. We are going to the Sinai Desert.

'You have five days to be ready to travel. I've been advised that the men are trained and ready and the horses are in good condition.'

Captain Carlsone said to his men, 'We'll have one last check of the horses – shoes, hoofs, eyes, teeth, skin and a quick canter to check their gait. We have nearly four hundred horses to check. You will inspect one hundred horses each. I'll handle any problems you find.

'Try to keep the inspection of each horse to a maximum of fifteen minutes. We should complete the inspection within three days.'

The horses had been tied in rows, to what were called picket lines. Each Horseman had his saddle and equipment in front of his horse. The four of them inspected down the picket lines without missing a single horse.

They completed the inspection on target and found only a few items of concern, mainly horseshoes showing considerable wear. They were replaced immediately.

The Light Horsemen were basically mounted infantrymen and in action they would dismount and use their rifles and bayonets. One Horseman would tend the horses while the three others would fight. The Horsemen slept near their horses in bell shaped tents. Eight men to a tent, with their feet facing inwards.

The departure day arrived with the brigadier leading the long columns of Light Horsemen riding three abreast, followed by their support parties. Jackson relished the sight and felt proud to be one of them. His team followed the 4TH Light Horse Regiment. The brigade looked efficient and capable.

The brigade headed due east towards the Suez Canal.

The Australian Navy's bridging party had built several temporary bridges over the Suez Canal for ease of movement into the Sinai Desert. The sun was now high in the sky, and it was hot, bloody hot. Halts were called every few hours.

They were adjacent a railway line and a water pipeline. Water was of concern for the columns in the immediate future and essential prior to battle.

Jackson being a Roman Catholic was familiar with the names on their maps. They were well-known names in the bible. He mused he had never expected that one day he would be riding in these fabled lands. Famous biblical town names such as Bethlehem, Jerusalem, Nazareth, Damascus and even Beersheba.

The sight of Australian Light Horsemen riding camels was a surprise. Out of the sands of the desert came a long line of the Camel Corp. These slow-moving animals could go for days without water, their large feet helping to spread their weight on the soft, loose sand. But they still moved faster than infantrymen and could carry large loads.

Jackson knew very little about camels and was hopeful he would not be asked to inspect them. All he knew was that they spat and liked to bite people.

Jackson could imagine how these animals would be used before the time of Christ. The desert Arabs would have had them as their only reliable transport from oasis to oasis, crossing the endless dunes.

Mules were only five feet high and would have been of more use in the towns and be easier to stable in an ordinary house, rather than finding a stable for an eight feet high camel.

The horse and the camel were integral parts of the desert offensive. The camel could carry large loads, but the horses could move faster over large distances. The infantryman could do neither. The three complimented each other in their endeavours and objectives.

As they rode, Jackson asked his sergeant, 'How long have you been with the Light Horse?'

He answered, 'When we were split up, we were going to France but when we reported for duty in London, we were kept at a training camp for a short time. Then they said they knew our background and we were to be sent to Egypt to join the 3rd Light Horse Brigade. In 1916 the Turks tried to strike across the Northern Sinai.

'The Mounted Division stopped them at Romani in August 1916. This was the start of the Desert Campaign. Basically, we were mounted infantry. Early 1917 we were formed to lead the Allied drive to Palestine.'

The sergeant continued talking. 'The Turks have a frontline of thirty miles, extending from Gaza to Beersheba. The infantry suffered several setbacks this year. Magdhaba and Rafa were won, but the next battles were not so successful.'

He looked at Jackson, who nodded to him to keep talking. 'I was transferred to the new 4th Regiment and here I am. The brigade comprises a New Zealand Rifle Corp and some other nationals. We're actually part of what is called the ANZAC Mounted Division. One thing has changed, we finally have an Australian commander, and he seems to think differently from the previous British incumbent. I don't think we will have the same disasters under his command as we did in Gallipoli and Europe.'

Jackson said, 'You will have some stories to tell your grandchildren.'

'Well, I hope you're right. This next battle is going to be big. So, I guess we're in for some excitement.'

The dust made by the horses was not very pleasant. It had some Horsemen sneezing and others coughing. Jackson had a dampened cloth tied around his face. Every few hours, a stop was called for a meal break and to water the horses.

An infantryman commented, 'You blokes seem to look after your horses better than yourselves.'

'Yes, they work harder than we do.'

That evening, the orders came down the line. In two days, they would be attacking Beersheba. They needed a good night's sleep as they would be travelling during the night.

The infantry had engaged the Turks first in the morning with no success. The Australian Light Horse commander had then called up the 4th Regiment to be ready to charge the Turkish defenders at the trenches.

Prior to the forthcoming battle. Jackson sat down and wrote to both Jane and Mary. He was uncertain what to write.

The coming battle was in the back of his mind. He wrote Jane's letter first. He felt his words seemed restrained. Normally, he wrote freely and without thinking. Tonight, he couldn't. Mainly, he just asked questions about what was happening in Riverbank.

Mary's letter was free flowing. He missed her company and told her of the loneliness, and of how at night, he would walk around the camp and look at the Sphinx and the Pyramid and think of her. He was missing home very much and company, particularly hers.

After riding through the night, they arrived at dawn. The regiment assembled several miles from Beersheba and was now in position to attack. The Turks had repelled the infantry all day. Time was now becoming critical as the horses needed water. It was now that the 4th Light Horse Regiment became cavalrymen. Victory was the only thing on the Horsemen's minds.

Beersheba was only a few miles away. The 4th Light Horse Regiment was on the left flank. They knew that there was no barbed wire in front of these trenches.

The regiment's Horsemen were roughly lined abreast for hundreds of yards. Bayonets, glinting in the sun, were drawn from their scabbards. They had been sharpened the night before. Some had their bayonets fixed on their rifles.

Who would have guessed the mounted infantry would become a cavalry? The horses were as restless as their riders. The Horsemen were nervously talking among themselves, waiting for the order to charge. The charge would be over a distance of a few miles.

The order to charge was given. Hundreds of Light Horsemen soon had their horses walking, then trotting, then cantering and finally the gallop. The Horsemen, using their initiative, spread out in a line and only moved inwards when they got close to the Turkish trenches.

Jackson and his team followed the centre line of the 4th Regiment's second line of Horsemen, only a few yards behind them.

His men had also sharpened their bayonets eager to be in the action. The sergeant had a bayonet and revolver while Jackson had a revolver.

The Turks had seen them coming and waited and waited and opened fire when the Light Horsemen were in range. Smoke was coming from the Turks trenches, artillery shells first, then machine gun bullets were whizzing over their heads. Some Horsemen were hit and fell from their horses. Horses also were hit by bullets and screamed as they fell mortally wounded. The noise was deafening from the thundering of hooves, shouting Horsemen, artillery and machine guns firing.

The charge continued unabated as they got nearer the trenches. Then the Horsemen were under the guns, two hundred yards from the trenches, the Horsemen started yelling louder. The speed of the charge had not allowed the Turks enough time to adjust their gun sights. Turks were now firing high.

The regiment's first line of Horsemen was now over the first trenches. The leading Horsemen jumped from their horses into the trenches. In their excitement, they were still yelling obscenities at the enemy. Hundreds of riders dismounted and began hand-to-hand fighting.

The regiment's second line continued to the next trench and engaged the Turks. Some Turks were killed with bayonets used as sabres. The Turks had used their bayonets thrusting them up into the horse bellies.

The surprise and speed of the attack had unnerved the Turks. The superior skills and determination in the hand-to-hand fighting and the use of the bayonets had the Turks surrendering. Soon the entire barracks surrendered. One Light Horseman had twelve Turks surrender to him. The battle for the Beersheba wells was over by 1750 hours. Unfortunately, as in all battles, there were casualties, thirty-one Light Horsemen were killed and thirty-two wounded.

Jackson had jumped over both trenches and followed the other Light Horsemen who were heading towards the town.

A Turkish soldier suddenly appeared around a corner. His horse reared up unexpectedly and stumbled. Jackson jumped clear as the horse fell. He leapt from his horse and at the same time, drew his pistol and shot and killed the Turk, just as the Turk fired his rifle and shot him in the left shoulder. Jackson knew he was in trouble when he couldn't raise his left arm. He walked to his horse as a major rode up.

'How bad is your injury? Can you ride?'

Jackson answered, 'Yes. If I can get up on my horse.'

The major helped him to mount and pointed to a large building in the distance. 'I'm going to take control of the building. By the time you get there, it will be a casualty ward. Good luck.' He then rode off at a gallop.

Jackson looked back at the trenches. He could see the Light Horsemen were winning. Many Turks were surrendering. He wondered, *Where are my men?* The dust in the air made it difficult to identify individuals as the sun was setting lower in the sky. It was almost impossible to determine who was who.

As Jackson rode slowly towards the town a mile away, he saw the water wells the Light Horse needed for their horses. The local population was subdued, wondering what the future held for them. Just as he reached the doorway of the building with the red cross, he collapsed and fell off his horse.

He woke up lying on a mattress on the floor of a large room. A voice said, 'Good. You're awake. What happened?'

'A rifle bullet at very close range,' Jackson replied.

The doctor said, 'At first inspection, the damage is soft tissue only. We think the bullet missed the bones. But we're not sure. It will be quite some time before the swelling goes down. You've lost a lot of blood, but you'll feel stronger in a few days. You were lucky. Next week, you'll be on a ship to England. Goodbye and good luck.' The doctor went to the next wounded soldier.

The next day Jackson was sitting outside on a box waiting to be picked up and taken to the railway siding. The General-in-Command rode by with his regiments following him.

As they triumphantly entered the town, a voice suddenly called out, 'Good to see you again, sir.'

He looked up to see one of the original troopers of his first squad waving to him. Unfortunately, they would not be able to meet this time. Hopefully they would all meet again.

All he could do was to wave back and loudly call, 'Good luck.' Another one of his troopers was still serving.

The trip to the railway siding was uncomfortable in the horse-drawn ambulance wagon. The driver had done two round trips that day to the railway siding via the camp to bring other wounded soldiers into the temporary town hospital. The train trip was smooth but sweltering.

Looking out of the window at the desert, he wondered how the nomadic tribes had survived for centuries in this barren land. Every now and then an oasis would appear in the distance with its green palm trees and colourful tents and, of course, some camels.

The desert towns all had a sameness about them – square buildings made with sandstone or a mixture of sand and animal dung. Camels and donkeys were the main source of travel. Roads were few and far between towns. Jackson's shoulder was painful but tolerable; he could still sleep.

To be in an area with so much history and miss touring them was disappointing, but so be it. From the times of Christ through to the Crusades and the creation of the Ottoman Empire, the associated biblical towns were all around him. His wound prevented him from enjoying any of these historical towns.

The sergeant went looking for Jackson without success. He would remain with the 4th Light Horse Regiment and be with them when they first rode into Jerusalem, ending the four-hundred-year rule by the Ottoman Empire.

CHAPTER SEVENTEEN

Mary Again

Jackson's ship sailed nonstop to Plymouth. It was smooth seas the entire trip. Even the English waters were calm for a change. He had written a letter to Mary.

He would only post it when he knew to which rehab he was being sent. His shoulder had improved dramatically. The swelling had gone down, but he still had trouble moving his upper arm. The wound was still tender to touch and inflamed.

Fortunately, his rehab was only twenty miles from Mary's rehab. Two weeks later Mary made a surprise visit.

She said, 'People will talk about us if we keep meeting like this.' She leant over and kissed him.

Jackson replied, 'Let them. It's good to see you again. I received one of your letters when we were in the Sinai desert.'

She asked, 'What was it like in the desert?'

He answered, laughing, 'Bloody hot and sandy. I thought you might have been posted home by now.'

'Well, I've been told I will be going home on the next rotation, but I've been told that before. We are very short of nurses!'

Mary organised a wheelchair and the two of them sat in the park and chatted, as would good friends. They talked of home, the war, the food shortages and naturally, the English weather.

The afternoon went quickly, and it was soon time for Mary to leave. She asked, 'Has the doctor told you you might be discharged soon. Your bed chart states that they can do no more for you. There's no bone damage and the muscles are functioning correctly. All they can do is "recommend specific exercises". I think they'll discharge you within the week.'

Jackson nodded. 'I was going to ask that question next time the doctor does ward rounds. I'll try to get some leave before I'm posted to wherever. Perhaps we can spend some time together.'

Mary smiled. 'I'd like that. I'll have to go. I'm on night duty at 2000 hours.' She wheeled him back to his bed, kissed him goodbye and departed.

Two days later the doctor came to see him. 'Good morning, captain. I have good news for you. You're going to be discharged tomorrow. To obtain full use of your upper arm, you will be required to do specific exercises. You will be given an exercise booklet when you are discharged. Also, you will be given your file documents and a leave pass for seven days. Then you sail for Australia.'

He thanked the doctor and his staff for their attention to his wound and for the good news.

He was back in unform again, complete with the emu feather in his hat. He was now Captain Carlsone

M.C. again. When he visited Mary at her rehab hospital, he waited in the staff room for her. He wore the blue patch on his arm signifying he was a wounded soldier recuperating. When Mary arrived, she was in her outdoor uniform. He realised then this was the first time he had seen her in uniform. She looked very smart and professional, and he complimented her on her appearance.

She smiled. 'You look rather smart yourself with your emu feather in your hat.' She put her arm in his as they walked down the street. An Australian newspaper photographer saw them and asked if he could photograph them. They happily agreed. This opportune photograph was to be circulated throughout Australia by the majority of the state's newspapers.

A photograph of an Australian Light Horseman awarded a Military Cross who had been wounded twice, together with an Australian nurse, both who had seen service in Gallipoli. This photograph was what the Australian politicians and people wanted as a morale booster.

Two days later, Mary and he were in uniform, walking past a pub, when a drunk staggered out the door and looked at them. 'What are you? A fairy soldier?'

Jackson ignored him, but the drunk continued to follow them. 'Go on, walk away. You're a coward and take your ground sheet with you.'

Mary could see Jackson was getting angry. 'Ignore him. Take no notice of him.'

Jackson ignored her request and turned to the drunk. 'Bugger off or else.'

The drunk said, 'Or else what? You've got an arm in a sling. What can you do?'

Jackson walked up and punched the drunk hard in the face with his right hand, not once but three times in quick succession. The drunk staggered and then slowly collapsed to the ground.

A crowd had gathered as four other Australian soldiers walked over. A constable then arrived on the scene. He looked down at the drunk who was bleeding profusely from his nose and mouth.

He asked the drunk, 'What happened to you?'

He mumbled something about 'Australia'.

The constable walked to the four Australian soldiers and asked, 'Which one of you did this to him?'

The Australian soldiers answered, 'We weren't here. The fight was over when we arrived.'

The constable then asked, 'Did anyone see the fight?'

Several bystanders stepped forward and said, 'It was the soldier with his arm in the sling.'

'Is this correct, sir?'

Jackson answered, 'Yes, I'm afraid so. He insulted this lady and myself and I retaliated.'

The bystanders all supported his comments.

The constable replied, 'You must have a good right hand. You've taught him a lesson in good manners. Good night.' The constable then turned and walked off into the night.

The week went quickly. They both could see their relationship was sincere. They had fallen in love, but Jackson was engaged, and he was honourable. They found it difficult, remaining just friends.

Mary found it very difficult. She felt she should tell him about her suspicions of Jane and Michael, but she was fearful of Jackson's reaction. Wisely, Mary decided to wait and see what happened when they were both home again. She would wait for him and hope.

Jackson had been overseas for over three years and had been wounded twice. He had been given the all-clear from the UK rehab doctor with his latest wound. His shoulder now had ninety-five per cent mobility and he was being sent home for rest and recuperation.

The voyage back home was a mixture of both anticipation and regret. Jane or Mary? He was in a quandary. Could you love two people at once? He had not seen Jane for a long time. Would they both still feel the same about each other, the way they did before he left for overseas?

CHAPTER EIGHTEEN

Homeward Bound

The return voyage went quickly. He slept and read anything he could find on board to help pass the time. The ship stopped at Cairo to embark other soldiers returning home and then they went nonstop to Melbourne.

When they reached the heads at the entrance to Port Phillip Bay all the returning military personnel came out on deck to see the bayside towns. They enjoyed the simple sights – houses with smoke emanating from their chimneys, vehicles of all types driving on the bayside roads and people going about their daytime jobs. They were home again. It took several hours before they docked, but very few left the ship's guardrails. They wanted to enjoy seeing Australia again, albeit Melbourne.

The ship docked early on a Friday morning. The army had organised a parade for the next day. The service personnel had no interest in the march, but the politicians wanted the publicity and for civilians to see hundreds of marching soldiers who had fought overseas in war zones.

All the soldiers wanted to do was to go home to their families and forget the war, if possible. But first they went to the army barracks to obtain a train ticket and their back pay.

The parade was through the main streets of Melbourne and most of the office workers waved and threw streamers from their windows, while the shoppers cheered and waved. The war was nearly over and more and more service personnel would soon be returning.

Jackson was required to debrief at Victoria Barracks after the march through Melbourne. He was surprised to see so many army officers at the debrief. Jackson had not realised his experiences in the three theatres of the war and in England had been unusual. He was highly regarded in the War Office as an experienced and capable line officer. They wanted him to speak and answer questions from these new officers who were due to be posted to the current European battle areas. The debrief took two hours of questions and answers and left him almost exhausted.

Following a round of applause, the colonel thanked him and then gave him the good news he had been promoted to the rank of Major. More applause. Finally, he was given his new orders. He was to report to Broadmeadows Camp in fourteen days. The army still needed him.

He had written to Jane telling her he was on his way home. However, the letter was on the same ship he was travelling on. He would arrive home before the letter reached Jane. The first train to Riverbank was a freight train. He and two other soldiers talked the guard into letting them get in his van at the end of the train. It was uncomfortable but they would be home earlier. The train arrived at Riverbank at 0900 hours Sunday morning.

He walked to his uncle's place adjacent the station first, changed into civilian clothes and stowed his kit in the old barn. His aunt and uncle were not home; they would be at church.

He saddled a horse and rode out to Jane's farm. He would wait for her if she was at church. He waved to two farm hands as he dismounted. He noticed they continued to look at him.

He opened the front door and went to Jane's bedroom. Upon opening the door, he stopped, not believing what he was seeing – Jane and Michael, in bed naked.

Jane reacted first. White faced she leaped from the bed, breasts bouncing. She knew this was trouble. She pleaded with Jackson, screaming, 'No don't.'

Jackson backhanded her and she fell back semi-stunned.

Michael dodged around the bed and ran out of the house, stark naked.

Jackson caught him and began to thrash him. Twice he let Michael get up, then he punched him several times again. Michael finally collapsed, unconscious, bleeding profusely from his nose and mouth. One eye was swollen, and a cheekbone was dented.

The two workers grabbed Jackson and stopped him from continuing the assault.

In a daze, Jackson mounted his horse and rode back towards home. He walked to the river nook and looked at the water flowing by. His two so called "best friends". He didn't know how long he sat there.

He heard some people coming. They stopped and looked at him, one was the local police sergeant.

He sat beside him and said, 'What a welcome back, Jackson! I've heard of the trouble up at the Morris farm. Are you all right?'

He looked at the sergeant and answered, 'What do you think? I've been overseas for nearly four years, and I come home to this.'

The sergeant nodded. 'I'm sorry but I have to arrest you for assault. Will you come with me?'

Jackson stood up. 'Let's go.'

By noon Monday, half the town knew versions of the altercation at the Morris farm. Both Jane and Michael were taken to hospital.

Jane had a broken nose. It could not be repaired completely; it would always have a bend in it. She was home in three days.

Michael had a broken eye socket, a broken jaw, a depressed cheek bone and had lost four front teeth. He was destined to be in and out of hospital for a long time. His face was scared for life.

When the police started investigating the reasons behind Jackson's assault charge they were unable to find anyone who would speak against Jackson. When they interviewed the victims, even they were reluctant to say too much. The only witnesses, the workmen at the Morris farm, spoke out and said what they saw regarding Michael's assault. Jane sacked them the next day and they left the district.

Jackson was charged with common assault and bailed on his own recognisance. He was to be confined to his uncle's property, pending the trial.

Michael had been on a downhill road for several months. His health was of concern as he had not enjoyed a good night's sleep for quite some time and his diet left a lot to be desired. The worse of his problems was his business.

His debts had got out of hand. He owed the captain for the dubious goods he had purchased from him. His mortgage payments with the bank were behind and he was overdrawn on his business account. The locals refused to deal with him.

His business was bankrupt, and the family property and furniture auctioned. Jane refused to see him anymore, so he moved to Melbourne to his parents' house.

His parents were furious with him. 'How could you do that to your best friend and with his fiancée? Shame on you. You've lost our business in Riverbank. What were you thinking? You're a bloody fool! What are you going to do now with your life?'

'I need help,' Michael replied.

His father said, 'First, you need to start accepting responsibility for your actions.' He turned and left the room, slamming the door.

The court case was scheduled to be held in a week. The townspeople all wanted to get a seat in the courtroom. It was impossible, so the mayor had all the windows removed and the doors were kept wide open.

The magistrate was a country man with old values. The trial would not be by jury. He would decide the verdict. On the surface it appeared an easy case. Jackson pleaded guilty of assaulting Michael Rawley.

Jackson had not even retained a lawyer; he seemed to have lost interest in everything. He was still shocked by what he had seen.

The prosecutor was late arriving and was not fully briefed on the case by the local sergeant. The clerk read out the charge. Jackson pleaded guilty. The two witnesses were called, but they were not in court; they were in Queensland and staying there. However, they had signed their witness statements.

The magistrate instructed the prosecutor. 'If you have no more witnesses, call the victim and let's hear what he has to say.'

The prosecutor asked Mr Rawley, 'Can you tell us what lead up to this altercation?'

He didn't answer.

The magistrate looked at Michael. 'If you do not answer, I will gaol you. Do you understand?'

Michael nodded. 'We had a disagreement, and he is a better fighter than me and I lost.'

The magistrate said, 'That is not what you were asked. What was the disagreement?'

Michael hesitated.

The prosecutor then continued. 'The report says you were naked.'

There was an audible buzz from the onlookers. Mr Rawley was not acting like a victim. 'Was there a woman involved?'

Michael nodded.

'Was she your girlfriend or someone else's?'

The crowd murmured.

'Did Captain Carlsone start the fight?'

Michael replied softly, 'Yes.'

'Is the lady in court today? Is she a friend of Captain Carlsone?'

A voice in the crowd outside yelled, 'She is his fiancée.'

The magistrate asked Michael, 'Is this true?'

Michael was bent over and just nodded, without looking up.

The magistrate sat there for a moment then called the sergeant over. 'Do you have a copy of the alleged offender's army records with you?'

'Yes. I'll get them for you.' He handed them to him.

The magistrate called the prosecutor over and showed him a particular page. He said, 'I have sat on the bench for many years and today I wish I wasn't here. Captain Carlsone, please stand. I see you have served in Gallipoli, France and Palestine; you have been wounded twice and have been awarded the Military Cross. I salute you, sir.

'Were you at Beersheba?'

'Yes, I was wounded there.'

'I see you also have three unsolicited character references from a brigadier and two colonels.'

The crowd cheered.

'But the law is the law, and I must find you guilty of assault. As you have pleaded guilty, I have no choice but to sentence you to a minimum of twelve months' gaol. I believe a grave injustice has occurred here today and that you are the victim in this sordid episode.' He stood up and left the courthouse.

Jackson was handcuffed and taken to the local police cells where he would stay until the Black Maria police vehicle arrived to take him to gaol in Melbourne. There was silence in the courthouse. Jackson going to gaol – unbelievable!

Michael was a forlorn figure, left sitting by himself. He was absorbing the look Jackson gave him as he left the dock. He knew he must never meet Jackson again. He believed he would kill him.

* * *

Jane stayed at the family farm and rarely went to Riverbank. Small towns have long memories. She would never be able to forget what she had done to Jackson. Every time she looked in a mirror, she would see her bent nose.

The farm kept her occupied, but she missed going into town and to events like the local agriculture show. Her previous acquaintances no longer visited her, nor was she invited to visit them. The local residents could and would not forgive a fiancée who cheated on a war hero who had been wounded twice while he was serving overseas in Gallipoli, France and Syria. He had also been in the now famous Light Horse charge at Beersheba.

CHAPTER NINETEEN

Justice?

Sitting in the cell in the Riverbank Police Gaol, Jackson stared at the ceiling thinking, *Why me? What did I do to deserve this?*

His uncle and aunty were allowed to visit him. His aunty was extremely upset when she heard the full story. She was going to give Jane a "Piece of my mind" until Jackson asked her not to go anywhere near her.

He brooded as he was locked up in the Riverbank cell for a week, waiting for a police vehicle called the Black Maria to take him to Pentridge Gaol. The vehicle stopped on the way to Melbourne to collect two other convicted prisoners. They had been found guilty of committing only minor offences of theft, but they were second offenders. Jackson did not speak with them, as he was apprehensive.

Pentridge had been built in the 1850's. It was made of blue granite stone and had several sets of enormous gates. It had an ominous air about it. He could see guard towers on each corner. When they arrived, they were searched and had their handcuffs removed. Jackson answered a few questions and was then given a prison uniform and escorted to a cell. It was a double cell with an inmate already occupying it.

He stood up, gave Jackson a quick once over and then introduced himself as Alan Strickland.

Jackson returned with his name.

Alan said, 'I'm in for a forged cheque. What are you in for?'

He answered, 'For assault and I got twelve months.'

Alan said, 'I'm due out in six months; I've done six already.'

Jackson asked, 'What's it like?'

'If you stay on side with the wardens and avoid the standover crims, you'll survive.'

Jackson asked, 'What do we do here?'

'Well, there are gardens, kitchens, laundries, metal work for Government jobs, cleaning, wood carting, painting the offices and a few others. They'll find a job for you. What do you do for a living?'

'I'm a vet, specialising in horses.'

'There are stables here. You might be lucky,' replied Alan.

As predicted by Alan, the next day Jackson was taken to the stables. The warden said, 'On our record sheet you are listed as a veterinarian.' He pointed to the stables. 'We have horses transiting here several times a week. Your job will be to feed, water and groom them and whatever else you decide they may need. Manage them as you think fit. The prisoner who is looking after them now is due to be released next week and is now working in the laundry. It's an easy job but sometimes it will take you all day to complete. I'll be checking on you. If you do your job properly, well and good, but if you don't, you'll be penalised severely. You can start work now.'

Jackson nodded agreement but said nothing and walked to the stables.

The stables were clean. They had obviously been raked that morning. There were twelve stalls with a small paddock alongside. The tack room had an assortment of saddles, bridles, heavy duty harnesses and an assortment of blankets. Three Black Marias were parked on one side. Six horses were in the stalls and none in the paddock. He filled their feed bins and water troughs and began to curry comb the one most in need of a good grooming. The tack room was clean and the harnesses, bridles and saddles had been well looked after; they were in good repair and condition.

With the job he had, he rarely met other prisoners during work hours and only saw them during mealtimes. Normally he sat with Alan; sometimes he sat with others but he did not enter into conversations. He became known as the "Quiet man".

Alan and he were walking to the mess hall one day when Alan accidentally bumped a much larger man.

Alan said, 'Sorry'.

But the big man asked, 'Why did you do that?'

Alan repeated, 'I'm sorry' and began to walk away.

The big man king-hit Alan, knocking him to the ground.

Jackson said, 'Leave him alone. He's already apologised to you.'

The big man turned to Jackson and swung a fist, hitting him on the shoulder and spinning him around.

Jackson's temper surfaced and he turned around fighting. He charged the big man and hit him in the face four times before the big man could retaliate.

The big man hit Jackson once before Jackson hit him viciously and hard to the jaw. The big man fell to his knee.

The wardens were about to stop the fight when the senior warden said, 'Let them continue. It's about time someone gave this standover bully a belting.'

The big man stood up and Jackson knocked him down again and he kept swing punches at him while he was on his knees.

The senior warden then stepped in. 'Break it up. Move on. Away you go about your business.'

Alan grabbed Jackson's arm, pulling him away from the fight.

The story of the fight soon spread throughout the gaol, about the "Quiet man".

The next day the big man approached Jackson. 'You're good. Let's shake hands. I've never been beaten before.' They shook hands. Jackson and Alan were never challenged again.

Jackson and Alan were very similar in height, weight and hair colour. They could have been taken for brothers.

Jackson eventually told Alan of the events leading to him being gaoled.

Alan noticed Jackson was paranoid with his wish to find and kill Michael. He had become a very dangerous man. Alan could see that if he found Michael, he would kill him, regardless of the consequences.

Since Jackson had stood up for him, their friendship had reached a stage where Alan agreed to help Jackson find Michael.

Michael described Riverbank and Michael's business. He told him where to find Jane's. He described the appearances of both Michael and of Jane. He said nothing of Mary.

Alan was a remittance man. He had a steady income from his parents in England. He had no need to work.

His parents are wealthy landowners who paid him to remain in Australia. Alan had been in trouble with the daughter of a Lord High Chief Justice who swore he would have him gaoled if he ever returned to England.

CHAPTER TWENTY

Friends No More

Several returned service personnel had arrived back in Riverbank. One of them was Nurse Mary Giles. When Mary arrived home, a farm worker advised that her parents were in Melbourne for the week.

On a spur of the moment decision, she decided to visit Jane, unaware Jackson was in gaol.

Jane saw her riding up and waved to her. After the normal chit chat, Mary noticed Jane had changed. Apart from her mishappen nose, she was much more reserved, and she felt as if she were intruding.

Mary asked her straight out. 'You've changed, Jane. What's happened?"

Jane took a deep breath and told Mary of the whole sordid saga with Jackson in gaol for twelve months.

Mary was speechless. Jackson in gaol! No wonder she had not received any mail. She stood up, furious, and walked from Jane's farmhouse looking straight ahead. She mounted her horse and rode home.

Jane would not forget the look on Mary's face – shock, disbelief and anger.

When Mary got up and left abruptly, Jane knew Mary would never forgive her for allowing this to happen. She burst into tears, sobbing uncontrollably.

Mary went to the local police station and asked where Jackson was.

The police sergeant answered, 'Pentridge Gaol in Coburg on the northern outskirts of Melbourne.'

She would write to him. Overseas, she had lived every day waiting to see him again and she was not about to give up on him now. That night she sat up late trying to put words on paper. She chose her words carefully, as she had previously thought something was occurring between Jane and Michael. Should she have told Jackson of the possibility? She would have put herself in the firing line of his dangerous temper.

Mary started writing. Firstly, she stated her surprise of the events that had occurred. Secondly, she made the point that the incident in no way would affect her relationship with him. Thirdly, she wrote that she would be there for him when he was free. Fourthly, she wrote that she would visit him each month.

Mary then wrote about her family, the farm and that she had joined the district hospital. Because of her overseas experience she was now the second-in-charge of the emergency ward. She finished her letter with, *I am looking forward to your return letter.*

The following week Mary was walking down the main street when she was confronted by Michael.

He greeted her, 'Welcome back.'

Mary looked at him and then smacked him hard in the face. She turned and walked away without saying a word.

An elderly lady saw this and shouted, 'Cop that, you bastard. Good one, Mary.'

Michael was shocked. He now began to realise the depth of hatred some local people had for him because of his betrayal of a trust.

Michael had been drinking most of the afternoon in the local pub. He sat in a corner mumbling to himself. The barman eventually asked him to leave. Michael was in a nasty mood. The barman was bigger and, when he refused, the barman threw him out by his collar and waist belt. He landed on his shoulder, screaming abuse at him.

The barman looked at him. 'You're barred. Don't come back.'

Michael staggered to his feet and walked away, mumbling.

During the trial, he had been living in a shed at the back of his previous business. He still had the horse he had ridden from Melbourne, one of his few remaining possessions. He sat there, his anger building.

Jane had hurt him by refusing to have anything more to do with him. Foolishly, he now decided to visit her. He saddled his horse and rode to her farm. The sun was setting, and her two new workmen were sitting outside their bunk house having a beer. They nodded to each other. The workmen knew the story of him and Jane, and they were curious as to why he was there.

Jane was preparing her bath. As she had told Michael previously, she did not want to meet him ever again. When he walked into the house, she was totally unprepared for him.

'Get out. I don't want you anywhere near here, ever again.'

He just laughed at her. 'Well, I'm here now, back in our little love nest. Have you forgotten so soon? I can remember when you wanted me. Have you such a short memory?'

He moved towards her and grabbed her, forcing her onto the bed. He was too strong and as he began to open her dress, she screamed. He didn't stop. Her dress and under garments were torn open, exposing her breasts.

As he tried to kiss her breasts, Jane screamed and yelled, 'Stop. Get off me.'

The two workmen heard her screaming and went running into the bedroom to manhandle him off her, slamming him into the wall face first.

In his drunken haze, he hardly felt the impact. They took him from the bedroom, allowing Jane to regain her modesty by straightening her clothes.

The workmen waited on the veranda for Jane to compose herself. 'What do you want us to do with him?'

She said, 'Just get him out of my sight.'

The workmen let Michael go. Fortunately, Jane's mother took powerful sleeping tablets and did not hear the commotion.

The next day, Jane had recovered somewhat from the ordeal, although she was still a little shaken. What if the workmen had not been there? She went to the police and formally made a complaint against Michael.

The sergeant was undecided as to what the charge should be – assault or attempted rape? Her history with Michael clouded the incident somewhat.

Jane was firm. 'I want him charged with attempted rape.'

The two workmen agreed with Jane.

When the sergeant went to find Michael he was long gone.

The sergeant wrote out his report and forwarded it to Ballarat Police Headquarters where it came to the attention of Chief Inspector Gemini.

He realised it was the same Michael Rawley involved in the livestock investigation.

Michael had vanished. A warrant was issued for his arrest. Police stations throughout Victoria and New South Wales border towns were given his description and bulletins were displayed on post office notice boards.

Without any friends, Michael decided he would leave and never return to the district. Hopefully he could start a new life and put the memory of his folly behind him and hopefully avoid meeting Jackson after his release from gaol.

Mary was invited to the welcome home function, along with several other veterans. Her parents encouraged her to go. They were proud of her being a Gallipoli veteran. One of the soldiers had served in both Gallipoli and France, the others had endured the horrors of the battles in France and Belgium.

The mayor opened the evening by acknowledging them individually.

The veterans each made short replies thanking their families for their letters and parcels and the charities for their socks, scarves etc. and food parcels. The mayor wisely mentioned those who could not be here tonight.

Mary shed a quiet tear, as did a few others. They all knew to whom he was referring. Each veteran was presented with an embellished scroll. Dinner followed and then some dancing. Mary left quietly, going home with her parents.

When he received Mary's letter, Jackson was elated. But he was like her, wondering how to reply. He did not wish to discuss the incident. Finally, he decided to just ask questions regarding her family, farm and job.

Since he had been in gaol, he had spent the majority of the time thinking about his future. Unfortunately, his conviction had finished his military career. It was ironic, just when he had been promoted to major. He could stay with his uncle in the horse-trading business, start a veterinary practice or a combination of both. He remembered talking this over with Mary when he was in rehab. The balance of his time was taken up thinking about paying back Michael. It was never far from his thoughts. He would find him one day.

It was three weeks before Mary received a letter from Jackson. She was delighted. She was concerned he might have become withdrawn and anti-social. He began by thanking her for her moral support and her offer to visit him. As she expected, he did not discuss the incident. He asked her about her job, and about the lamb drop. He had heard the price of wool was increasing each year. He wrote that his uncle was employing two extra stockmen to purchase farm horses for the district. The shortage of farm horses had been created by the demand by the military for the war. That demand had now almost stopped.

His letter continued, *I might even stay in Riverbank.* He asked her what she thought of his idea. Mary was pleased he had asked her this type of question. It meant he valued her opinion. It gave her a warm feeling. Perhaps there would be a future for them after this was all over.

Her first visit to the gaol was a momentous occasion. It had been a year since they had seen each other. Unfortunately, they were separated by iron bars, but they were able to talk face to face again. Mary was surprised at how well Jackson looked. He was suntanned, fit and healthy and most importantly, he was not depressed.

Could this be because each night he dreamt of what he would do to Michael when he found him? His uncle had also told him of the attempted rape of Jane. Jackson just shrugged his shoulders, when he was told of this. It didn't interest him. As far as he was concerned, she had burnt her bridges and there was no way back.

Mary and Jackson continued to write letters to each other. The bond they had established in England was strengthening, with Mary continuing her monthly visits to see him.

On the day Alan was due to be released, they agreed to communicate via Jackson's uncle's business address. They shook hands and agreed to meet within a week of Jackson's release at the Riverbank Hotel.

Alan travelled to Riverbank as a tourist. He booked into the local hotel for a week and hired a horse. He wandered around, casually asking about Michael and Jane.

Unfortunately, word got around that someone was asking about them. Jane shrugged her shoulders, 'So what'. She couldn't care less about what was going on around her. She knew she had committed the ultimate sin – betrayal of a trust. She must now live with its consequences.

Although Michael had vanished, Jane stayed to look after her mother and manage the farm.

Alan persisted with his search for Michael. His attempt to bribe the local postmaster was successful. He asked him to advise him of any letters received addressed to Jane's farm.

He said, 'She rarely receives any letters.' But Alan felt there would still be some communication between them. He was right. A letter arrived from Melbourne, but it had no return address. That left him wondering – where to now?

Jackson had obtained a reputation after the gaol fight.

A warden thought he knew Jackson. He approached Jackson. 'I feel I know you from overseas. Did you serve?'

'Yes, I was in the 4th Australian Light Horse Regiment.'

The warden said, 'So was I. Were you at Beersheba?'

He replied, 'Yes.'

'I remember you now. You were the vet officer. You and your team were inspecting our horses before the "charge". You wore a Military Cross ribbon. I know why you're here. Justice is blind sometimes. In your case it definitely was. If you need any help while you're here, let me know.

'I have a soft spot for people who have been penalised for a crime caused by another issue. There are a few others like you who do not deserve to be in here.'

Jackson had only a month more to serve when a fight started in the mess hall. It soon developed into a riot. Jackson was not in the mess room when it started. He was with the gaol governor discussing rebuilding the stables. They were over sixty years old, and the wooden stalls posts had rotted.

The gaol sirens were blaring. The cell doors were now all locked but many of the prisoners were still in the mess hall. The mess wardens had been overpowered and some security keys were now in the hands of a group of prisoners. It seemed a senseless move.

The prisoners could not reach the gates and the armed tower wardens controlled the open areas to the gates.

A small group of prisoners headed to the administration block and were intent on going upstairs to the governor's office.

Jackson saw them from the window as they ran across an open area. The wardens shot three of them, but four of them reached the administration block. It was lunch time and only a clerk was in the building plus one warden at the top of the stairs.

Jackson looked around for a weapon. He saw the fire hose on the wall. He grabbed it and said to the warden, 'We have a better chance of stopping them with this as they come up the stairs. When I say "Now!" turn the water valve on full bore.'

The four prisoners were running up the stairs looking down at the steps and did not see Jackson until he called, 'Now!' The pressure and volume of water knocked the four of them off their feet and tumbled them back down the stairs. By the time they were sitting up at the bottom of the stairs, the warden and the governor were aiming rifles at the four prisoners.

More wardens soon arrived and took them, drenched and looking sorry for themselves, back to their cells. They would be charged later. The riot in the mess hall fizzled out and no one was really hurt.

Jackson learned later that the four prisoners were in a group intending to capture the governor and hold him prisoner until the State Premier agreed to release them. They had started the riot in the dining room to create a diversion. There was no way the Premier was going to create a precedence of allowing prisoners to kidnap a senior public servant and use him as a bargaining tool for their release. It was never going to happen.

Immediately after the incident, access to the administration building was changed to be only via a guarded locked door.

Following the incident, Jackson was concerned about how his actions would be viewed by his fellow prisoners. He had no reason to worry. The big man supported his action and that was sufficient to keep him safe.

The governor was a fair man and treated the prisoners accordingly. They did not want the governor to think that the other prisoners were behind the attempted kidnapping, The prisoners who had attempted to escape were given beltings by their inmates for "rocking the boat". The fact that two prisoners were shot dead and one wounded, sent a strong message to the inmates.

Jackson was sent for by the governor. When he arrived at his office, he was surprised to see a gathering there.

The governor stepped forward and shook his hand. 'Good morning, Jackson.' He paused. 'Your involvement in my intended kidnapping has got to the newspapers. They know of your history and why you're here. They want to interview you. It's your choice. Do you want to or not?'

He answered, 'Governor, I'm happy for you to tell the reporters what happened here yesterday, and I'll answer questions, but only questions relevant to the attempted kidnapping.'

The governor replied, 'Gentlemen, you heard the conditions of the interview. Let's begin.'

The governor gave a good descriptive explanation of the saga.

A reporter asked Jackson, 'Why did you get involved?'

The answer was direct and simple. 'Because it was the right thing to do.'

The reporter continued, 'Do you expect to receive some time off your sentence?'

'No, I do not.'

He was then asked, 'But most people feel you were the victim, not the offender in your case.'

Jackson did not answer. The interview came to an abrupt end. He stood up and walked out of the office.

The next day the papers were full of the story of the kidnapping attempt. Jackson was called a hero for saving the day. However, all the reporters had dug up the story of his trial and the outcome. His service record and his Military Cross were not neglected. He was pleased the newspapers did not show him in a bad light.

CHAPTER TWENTY-ONE

The Hunt

The day of Jackson's release was upon him. The twelve months had passed quickly. He had made a few friends, including the big man. He said his farewells and went to the governor's office. They had become friends; often Jackson had tea with him. This time was different. The governor presented him with a gold watch suitably inscribed. 'Goodbye and good luck. You deserve some.'

 He caught the midday train to Riverbank, arriving early evening. He went to his uncle's home, where he was warmly greeted by him and his aunty. They were pleased to have him home again. He looked so well. They sat up talking until the early hours. No mention was made of Jane or Michael. Jackson slept peacefully even though it was a different bed from the one he had been sleeping on for the last twelve months.

Mary knew he was coming home but not the day nor the hour. She was sitting at the lounge window when she saw the solitary horseman riding up the lane leading to the farmhouse. It was Jackson; finally he was here. She rushed to the veranda and waved. He waved in return.

She tied his horse to the hitching rail as Jackson dismounted. They put their arms around each other and kissed passionately.

He stepped back and said, 'You will never know how much I have been looking forward to this moment.'

Mary replied, 'I've been counting the days in this last month. You must be enjoying your freedom.'

'Yes. It feels strange, but enjoyable. I won't ever be going back to gaol, regardless of what I do.'

Mary looked at him and wondered why he said that, then promptly forgot about it. They dined at her farm, and he stayed overnight in the guest's room.

After breakfast he said, 'I have a few things to sort out over the next few weeks, so you won't be seeing me for a while, but rest assured I'll be back. I'm not going to be separated from you again.'

The next day he went looking for Alan. Letters from him had been disappointing. Michael was elusive and would be more so now Jackson was out of gaol.

Alan had left an envelope for him at the hotel reception desk. He would be returning this afternoon.

Jackson decided to wait and read the newspaper while enjoying a beer or two.

Several people recognised him and said, 'Hello and welcome back.' He waved to them but did not engage in any conversation. He wasn't up to that yet. He needed more time to settle into his freedom.

Alan arrived back at the hotel as the sun was setting. They shook hands and exchanged some greetings.

Alan spoke first. 'So, you made it. How are you enjoying your freedom? I have good news and bad news. Jane is here but Michael has gone to Melbourne. Where? I don't know!'

Jackson asked, 'How do you know he's in Melbourne?'

'I asked the postmaster. He knew but not where in Melbourne. His parents are there, so we can start with them.'

They travelled to Melbourne, and, with a map of the suburbs, they started to identify the whereabouts of the saddlers, leather goods manufacturers and leather merchants. It was proving difficult to identify the number of these leather manufacturing businesses. Every suburb seemed to have two or three. Leather covered armchairs were all the rage and had created new leather businesses overnight.

A local stable owner told them Michael's parents' business was somewhere in Collingwood, one of the original Melbourne suburbs. He showed them a trade catalogue.

It was advertising leather goods with Rawley's Leather Goods trading address.

Alan approached Michael's father and asked to see Michael. His father said, 'Buggered if I know where he is. He was here last week. He received a letter and an hour later, he packed his bags and left without saying a word.'

Alan asked, 'Are there any other family members he may visit?'

'Yes, he has three uncles with farms along the Murray River in New South Wales.'

Three customers had walked into the shop and Michael's father said, 'Sorry, no more questions.'

Jackson wondered who the letter was from, and what was in it to cause him to run again. The answer was simple – the letter was from the local bank manager. He had been approached by a person who said he was a relative of Michael's seeking to deliver documents to him regarding an inheritance. The man was a creditor after Michael's address.

The bank manager was also after money owed by Michael and his letter had inadvertently tipped off Michael that someone was looking for him.

Michael was taking no chances and left his parents' home. Whether he was still in Melbourne or had headed for distant pastures was another question.

Jackson and Alan put their thinking hats on. Michael's only skills were in leather goods. They presumed he had gone bush. He could ride a horse. Perhaps, he was working on one of his uncle's farms. But where?

Jackson knew he had a favourite uncle with a property up north. They decided to ask around Melbourne first.

They visited all the saddlers and leather manufacturers if they knew or had met a Michael Rawley. Their search was without success. Some had bought saddles from him but hadn't seen him since. Others knew his parents through the industry and the Royal Melbourne Agricultural Show Leather Products Exhibitions.

Jackson and Alan decided to return to Riverbank. Jackson went to his uncle's business while Alan intended to get a job working on Jane's farm.

Alan had been a medic during the war but had not served overseas due to a hip injury during training. He still had minor restricted mobility.

Jackson made the point that they must not be seen together. They would only meet at night at the wharf at 2100 hrs on a Sunday night.

Alan rode up to the veranda and dismounted. An elderly lady nodded to him and said, 'Hello. Do I know you?'

'No, I'm new in town. I'm Alan Strickland. I'm looking for a job.'

She nodded. 'My daughter does the hiring. She'll be along soon. Were you a soldier? Many come by looking for work.'

Alan replied, 'Yes. I was in the medical corps and before that I was a gardener in the Botanical Gardens in Melbourne.'

A horse cantered up the lane with a woman rider. She waved as she rode up. She dismounted and said, 'Hello. What can I do for you?'

Her mother interrupted. 'This man is a gardener and medical man and he's looking for a job. What do you think? Remember what we were talking about last week.'

Jane looked at Alan. 'My mother needs help at times,' she said. 'We do need a gardener. We'll give you trial for a month. You can start tomorrow. There's a bunkhouse if you wish to stay at the farm. I'll see you then.' She turned and went into the house.

Her mother smiled. 'I think we will get on very well.'

Alan was surprised at Jane's confidence and her quick decision making.

Alan met with Jackson as planned and told him of his success at obtaining a job at Jane's farm.

He was left to make his own decisions with the gardens. They had been neglected for the last few years.

The layouts were still good. The main problems were the out-of-control weeds. They were strangling the bushes and the flowers. He started at one end of the garden and worked forward. Within a week he had made an obvious difference. He had only done a fifth of the work required to finish the garden. To provide a reason for her to keep him on, he had piled all the removed weeds in front of the weeded area.

Jane walked by one day when he was struggling with a large scrub.

She asked, 'How are you enjoying the gardening?'

Alan replied, 'It's a bigger job than I thought but it will look good when I've finished it.'

Jane said, 'I can see an improvement already. My mother looked after the garden before she had her stroke and I'm ashamed to say, I've had no interest in it until now. You have done an excellent job. I'm glad you came along looking for a job.'

Towards the end of the garden project, Alan volunteered to do the shopping and mail collection.

Jane agreed. She gave him the supplies list of requirements and told him to take the light four-wheeler, which only needed one horse.

While the supplies were being loaded, Alan collected the mail. There were three letters: one for Jane and one to her mother. The other one was an invoice. The handwriting was similar on both envelopes.

The next day, Alan went to empty the house garbage bins and found a crumpled letter from Michael to Jane's mother. She was obviously not interested in anything he had to say and had thrown the letter away.

Alan read the letter, but it gave no clue where he was. However, he did mention that the river was running fast for this time of the year. The only river running fast this time of the year would be the Murray River.

Jackson was pleased. Finally, they were homing in on Michael. At long last! They now knew he was somewhere on the Murray River.

Jackson had a photograph taken with Jane and Michael when they were children standing outside a homestead at a farm owned by an uncle of Michael's. He put it in his pocket. Perhaps it would jog someone's memory. They decided to work their way along the towns to the South Australian border.

The next day Jackson went to the old barn and collected his loaded service revolver. He stowed it in his saddle bag without telling Alan. He rode into town to meet Alan and tell him he wanted to leave the next day.

Alan went to Jane and apologised. 'I have to go away for a month or two. I have a family problem I have to sort out.'

Both Jane and her mother were disappointed that he was leaving but they told him he had a job on the farm if ever he wished to return.

Jackson and Alan packed and left the next day. They had no idea where Michael was, but they were intent on finding him.

If Michael had not panicked when he received the bank manager's letter, he would have been easier to find. Jackson and Alan would not have had to follow in his tracks for weeks. Fleeing so soon after gave him a good start on them.

When Michael received the letter from the bank manager, he immediately thought Jackson knew his address. Later, he realised if Jackson had known where he was, he would have arrived there before the letter. He saddled one of the horses and headed north. He had several relatives with large holdings along the Murray River.

The weather was warm, sunny and dry and the fields surrounded by dark green forests. The bushlands of Australia were a painter's dream. Cattle and sheep, dams and creeks completed the picture. The scenery helped Michael to forget his worries for a short time. He travelled northwest for several days. He crossed the Murray River, then he headed west to one of his uncle's holdings.

His Uncle George was his favourite. Although he hadn't seen him for several years, he knew he would be welcomed. He rode for two more days, sleeping under the stars. He avoided towns. The rape charge worried him. Would people in New South Wales country know?

Finally, he came to the sign, *Eureka Station*. He had arrived at long last. He was looking forward to a bath and a shave and a home cooked meal. As he rode up to the homestead, he saw several stockmen looking at him. He waved and they responded likewise. He asked, 'Is George around?'

One of the stockmen pointed to a large shearing shed. 'He's over there.'

Michael dismounted and led his horse to the shed, tying him to a hitching rail outside.

His uncle saw Michael enter the shed and did not recognise him at first. It was only when he said 'Hello, Uncle' that George realised who he was. 'Well, I didn't expect to see you here. I heard you had some trouble down south. Anyway, it's good to see you. How are your parents? I believe they have a successful business in Melbourne now.' They shook hands.

Michael answered, 'Yes. They are well and making money. I came here for a break from Riverbank.'

His uncle said, 'We heard it was girl trouble. You're not running from the law, are you?' If you are, we have a problem. The NSW police have already been here looking for you.'

Michael was dumbfounded. He had not expected this. He replied, 'Can I have a bath, a shave and a hot meal? I will go then, if you wish.'

His uncle nodded. 'Yes, I'm sorry but I think it's for the best. Go to Stan's place. It's in the middle of nowhere. You should be out of sight and safe from prying eyes in those thousands of acres.'

Michael rose from a good night's sleep, refreshed and ready to travel to his Uncle Stan's sheep station. George told him of the two ways to get to *Sunset Ridge*. The long trip was by a dusty cattle track road, but it meandered and took twice as long. The shorter journey was across country, very dry and barren of vegetation and could be done in four days.

George had travelled the shorter trip once. 'It's not easy but it can be done. Head for the Twin Peaks at all times. His homestead is at the base, in between them. We've packed you extra water, food and horse fodder with an extra horse. Good luck and say hello to Stan for me.'

Michael waved and, with a canter, he rode out leading his pack horse across the paddock towards the distant Twin Peaks. He had a quick stop every two hours to water the horses. The sun was unrelenting.

He stopped at a large dead tree around sundown. After watering and feeding the horses, he checked their hoofs and cleaned within their shoes. All looked good and their shoes were not loose.

The next day he started early to avoid an hour or so of sun exposure. He travelled quickly and then slowed down when the sun was overhead. Mid-afternoon he found some shade under an outcrop of rock and the horses and Michael had an early finish to their day. At all times he kept the Twin Peaks in sight. With his inexperience in this environment, they still seemed to be a long way away.

Day three loomed with strong gusty winds. He could see that this would be a very uncomfortable day for both him and the two horses.

He was heading into the wind and the dust it stirred up. The dust was in his eyes and made it difficult to see where he was heading. He tied a handkerchief over his mouth and nose, but he still tasted gritty dust. After a three-hour stint, he stopped and watered the horses and had a drink himself.

He continued for another three hours. He was unsure if he was heading in the correct direction. The wind was less intense, but he had lost sight of the Twin Peaks. He decided to stop overnight where he was, hoping the wind would abate by next morning. During the night, he heard the unmistakable howls of dingos. He had a rifle with him and was not concerned, but the horses were restless. Fortunately, the dingos did not come close. When the howling stopped, the horses settled down.

The wind dropped to a slight breeze the next morning. Michael was pleased he could see the Twin Peaks again. He had strayed to the north, but he didn't think he had lost too much time. Now back on track, he stepped up the pace to make up the lost time. He estimated he had sufficient water for three more days.

The trip had taken his mind off the reason he was going to his Uncle Stan's. He felt relaxed for the first time in many months. He was remorseful for his drunken attack on Jane.

He intended to write to both Jane and her mother, begging their forgiveness. Why had he been such a fool? Was it arrogance? Was it just plain lack of thoughtfulness by not respecting his long-time friends? He had betrayed Jackson's trust and now he was running from him. He was fully aware of his explosive temper. Michael thought he would probably be safer in gaol. Although, if he was gaoled for rape, maybe the other prisoners might give him a very hard time.

He came to a small dry creek bed. It had some brambles in the middle of it and as the pack horse walked by it, a snake struck its hind leg. The horse whinnied, Michael turned and saw a death adder slide out from under the horse. He continued up out of the creek bed, hobbled the horses and, armed with his rifle, he returned and found the snake still in the same position as before. He shot the head off the snake then went back to the bitten horse.

He intended to cut along the fang holes, but he was unable to find the fang marks. As he had no anti-venom, he continued the trek with the injured pack horse as before. He would just have to wait to see how much venom had been injected into the horse. Only time would tell. Michael did not want to kill the horse if it had a chance to survive the bite.

He soon had his answer. Within an hour the horse became distressed. It began to throw its head around and neigh.

Michael drew his rifle to put it down when it suddenly collapsed and died. When it fell, it split the last water bag.

Michael was angry with himself. He should have foreseen this possibility. He now had a problem. He only had two canteens of water remaining. He took the food and some fodder from the dead pack horse and left him. The eagles, crows, dingos and other wildlife would soon devour the carcass. Such is life in the outback.

Michael rode until the sun set. In the distance he could see a light. He could not guess how far. The next morning at sunrise he continued towards the Twin Peaks. At last, they seemed to be closer.

There were dust clouds on the horizon. Maybe a cattle muster? He was heading in their direction; hopefully he could meet them. He had run out of water yesterday afternoon and now both he and the horse were showing signs of weakness from dehydration. As they got closer to the dust cloud, he decided to fire a few rifle shots to see if he could attract their attention.

He continued riding towards the dust cloud. After half an hour he thought, *Well the shots weren't heard but I'll keep heading in their direction.* Suddenly two horsemen appeared on the horizon, riding towards him. He waved when they came closer.

The horsemen were stockmen. They rode with long stirrup leathers.

Michael dismounted. 'Did you hear my rifle shots.'

The stockmen answered, 'Yes. You're a long way off the beaten track. Are you lost?'

He replied, 'Yes and no. I'm heading to *Sunset Ridge*, my uncle's station. I lost my pack horse to a snake bite, and I ran out of water yesterday.'

The stockmen had dismounted. One gave Michael his water canteen, the other took off his hat and poured some water into it and held it for the horse to drink.

The taller of the two said, 'We're from *Sunset Ridge* and we're heading that way now. Follow us. We'll be there tomorrow around noon.'

Michael was now no longer concerned about finding his uncle's station. He wondered how Uncle Stan would greet him. Hopefully he would be unconcerned about Michael's alleged crime. Would a police visit be warranted out in this remote area? As he got closer to the homestead, he saw a small river and a pier. A paddle steamer was moored, and sheep were being loaded into its hold.

The homestead had been added to, as his uncle had prospered. It was large and rambling – three large sheds and several holding paddocks along each side of a small river.

He rode up to the homestead and knocked on the door.

A pleasant middle-aged woman opened the door. 'Hello, where did you spring from?'

He answered, 'I'm Michael Rawley from Riverbank.'

Just then a voice enquired, 'Who did you say you were?'

'Michael Rawley.'

'Well, I'll be blowed. Come in. This is a surprise. You're a long way from home.' Laughingly he asked, 'Are you on the run?'

Michael said nervously, 'No, I just needed to travel a little, too much work and all that.'

His Uncle Stan replied, 'Glad to have you. Stay as long as you like. We have plenty of rooms. Josie, my housekeeper, will show you around. I'll see you at dinner tonight. We'll talk then.' He turned and left the room.

Josie showed him to an upstairs room overlooking the river and the pier.

The river flowed slowly south to eventually join up with the Murray River. He was surprised that it was a subsidiary of the mighty Murray River.

After a few weeks, he began to feel safe until a friend, who was a riverboat crewman, told him of two men inquiring after him in a pub down river. The next day he boarded the river boat and left. He liked his uncle and would have stayed on as stockman. But now he had to leave.

He returned to Melbourne to stay with his parents until he found a job. In the back of his mind there was the very real possibility that Jackson would eventually find him. He stayed in their business premises during the day and, only on Monday nights, would he venture out and have a beer in a small local pub. The pub was virtually empty on Monday evenings.

Jackson was waiting outside the hotel and saw Alan riding towards him. He asked Alan, 'Are you packed yet?'

Alan nodded. 'Let's go.'

They rode out of town, heading west along the river. The day was cloudy and the wind crisp. They made good time to the next town. Most villages were about twenty-five miles apart. It was roughly the distance horse drawn coaches could travel between them in the 1800's. These villages began with a tavern or inn, then a shop, a blacksmith and a school. Suddenly, from a village some became towns.

They asked around for people named Rawley and showed the picture of the farmhouse to all and sundry. They travelled to six towns without any luck. At the seventh town, their luck changed.

A barman answered their query. 'I've heard of the Rawley's. George Rawley was a famous horseman. He came from further out west. He had a place near the river junction. Follow your nose for a day or two and you can't miss it. It's called *Eureka* something or other.'

They thanked the barman and left.

Jackson was delighted. At last some useful information.

They started early the next morning, hoping to reach the river junction by nightfall. But it was not to be. They stopped at a town for dinner and were told they still had ten miles to go, and the road was full of potholes. They agreed it wasn't worth risking the horses travelling in the dark just to save a few hours.

Rain arrived overnight and made the road even more dangerous. They rode cautiously, watching for puddles. The horses were avoiding them, without any help from their riders. They arrived at the river junction where there was a small inn.

They had been riding for a few hours, so a tea break was due. The inn owner knew Richard Rawley. He collected his mail there once a week. The name was *Eureka*; he didn't know why.

Jackson asked, 'Has anyone else been by here lately? I thought his nephew was coming to visit him and we're friends of his.'

The owner shook his head. 'No, no one I don't know has been past here in the last week.'

He pointed to the road on the other side of the river and said, 'Follow that road for about five miles until you come to a road off to the left. You'll see a sign to Tuwala. It's twenty miles straight on. Goodbye. I've work to do.'

'Let's hope we can make Tuwala by nightfall. At least the rain has stopped,' Alan commented. He looked at Jackson. He had noticed he was getting animated, unable to sit still and, at times, seemed vague. He knew Jackson hated this man, but he now started to wonder what the end result was going to be.

They arrived at Tuwala late afternoon. After a lot of persuasion, Alan convinced him to stay in town and visit *Eureka Station* the next morning when they were fresh.

After dinner they adjourned to the bar where Jackson began talking to the barman.

The barman asked, 'Are you staying for long or just passing through?'

'I came up here as a schoolboy and stayed at *Eureka*. I'm in the district and thought I would drop in. Here's an old photo when I was here last.'

The barman looked at it. 'It hasn't changed much, only the trees and scrubs are much bigger.'

Jackson could hardly contain his delight. This was the farm he had been searching for these past weeks. Tomorrow would be a big day.

Alan was apprehensive. He was not looking forward to it at all.

At breakfast Alan asked Jackson what he intended to do if, and when, he found Michael was at the farm.

He did not answer.

The ride to *Eureka* was in silence and it seemed to take forever.

Twice Wounded

The sign over the entrance told them they had arrived. Nestled in the tall trees was the homestead. As the barman said, the building was the same as he remembered it as a young boy. A man was standing on the front veranda with his thumbs in his trouser braces.

He politely asked, 'Who might you be?'

'I visited here as a young boy with Michael Rawley. I was in the district, and I thought he was visiting you, so I decided to drop in.'

He replied, 'I'm George, his uncle. Yes, Michael was here but I told him to go. I think he is running away from the law.'

Jackson was stunned. He believed he would find Michael here.

Alan asked, 'Where did he go?'

George answered, 'I don't know, and I don't care. Good afternoon.' He turned and walked to the door and went inside the homestead.

Jackson, surprisingly, quickly recovered from his disappointment. He knew there were three brothers – George, Richard and Stan.

At the next town they approached the postman. Richard had moved from the district to further up the Murray River towards the border. He was near a weir and had decided to grow fruit and vegetables. He shouldn't be too hard to find.

They kept riding until sunset when they came upon a wayside inn. Dinner and then a good night's sleep was the order of the day. Next day at sunup, they were off again.

The postman was right – at the next town they saw a large notice board advertising Rawley products for sale. The address showed the farm was only a day's ride away. A chance meeting with a police constable surprised them.

'Oh, yes, I know two of the Rawley brothers. Chalk and cheese, they are. Richard is a law-abiding citizen and the other, Stan, we suspect of rustling sheep and cattle along the river. Richard is a pillar of society, Stan a suspect in local crime. He lives inland at the base of the Twin Peaks on a river.'

Jackson hoped this visit to Richard Rawley would be successful. He still had a burning hatred in him to ultimately kill Michael.

He still had memories of that day. Full of optimism, they rode out following the noticeboard's directions. They arrived late in the afternoon and camped out alongside the river.

Sleeping under the stars on a clear night and enjoying the quietness and solitude, Alan was at peace with himself, but he doubted if Jackson was of the same mind.

They were woken by a noisy kookaburra, laughing his head off. Then a second bird started. Very soon the trees echoed with their laughter.

While Jackson boiled the billy for tea, Alan sat looking at the river waters flowing by. The towering gum trees completed a typical Australian bush scene.

The road to Richard's farm was easy to follow and they timed their arrival for around noon. The road went between paddocks that were lush with all types of vegetables. In the distance, they could see several large orchards. When they called at the farmhouse, no one answered. They then rode over to a very large barn and saw several people loading crates full of their local produce.

A young girl said, 'Good morning. Can I help you?'

They both dismounted. 'Hello. We're friends of Michael Rawley and we believe he's visiting here. I presume this is Richard Rawley's farm.'

She answered, 'Yes, this is my father's farm but Michael's not here. We haven't seen him for years.'

Disappointed, Jackson said, 'I was told he was coming to visit his uncle.'

The girl replied, 'There are two other uncles, Uncle George and Uncle Stan up on the branch river near the Twin Peaks.'

Just then a middle-aged man walked up. 'I'm Richard Rawley and I heard your conversation. I think Michael was in some trouble assaulting a woman. He wouldn't come here. I don't condone that type of behaviour. Do I know you? You look familiar.'

Jackson queried, 'Well, he said he was going to see an uncle up on the river.'

Richard persisted, 'What's your name?'

'I'm Jackson Carlsone and this is Alan Strickland.'

Richard said 'Yes, I remember you now. You're the Military Cross winner from Riverbank.'

Jackson nodded and moved to mount his horse.

Richard said, 'Sorry we can't help you, but try Stan's place over at Twin Peaks. Follow the road north. It's a long ride, but you can't miss it.'

They mounted their horses, waved goodbye and rode back towards the river.

Alan suggested they go and have a talk with the constable again and ask him the best way to travel to Stan Rawley's station.

The constable looked up. 'How did you go?'

Jackson replied, 'No good. He wasn't there. He suggested we try his brother's place at Twin Peaks. What's the best way to get there?'

The constable called to a stockman near the door. 'What's the best way to get to Stan Rawley's station?'

The stockman walked over. 'It's a bugger of a trip. That country is dry and dusty. Are you after a job?'

'No, we're looking for someone.'

'Well, he hasn't hired anyone for over three months. The only visitor lately is his nephew. A bit of a bludger; he doesn't like work.'

Jackson could hardly contain himself. He asked, 'What does he look like?'

The stockman described Michael exactly – height, build, eyes and hair colour.

'What's the best way to get there?'

He pointed towards the river road. 'Follow that road until you see the Twin Peaks Road and a sign *Sunset Ridge*. It will take you to Stan's station. It's a long way – four to five days. It's dry out there, so take plenty of water. Watch out for snakes. There are some real bad buggers in the dry scrubs.' He nodded and walked away.

The constable said, 'He knows this country. He was born here. If you're not back here within two weeks, I'll come looking for you.' They thanked him for his help and left to prepare for, hopefully, the end of their search. There was not a cloud in the sky. The sun blazed down on them without mercy.

When they left the river flats, the country gradually became drier and drier. At times, small dust eddies would spiral and spin towards them, enveloping them in the dust they carried. The dust was gritty and stung their eyes. They needed a damp cloth to wash their eyes. At times they stopped to check their horses' eyes too.

The news that Michael was at last located put a spring in Jackson's step.

Alan still wondered what was going to happen when the two of them met up again.

Sleeping out at night in this dry country was not as comfortable as the riverbank. The noises were different. In the night the dingos would howl; in the morning there was the cawing of the crows.

The ride was monotonous. They would stop every few hours where there was some shelter from the sun. Water was a concern. They had weighed the horses down with as much water as they could carry.

On and on they travelled. Jackson began to appreciate how much of a friend Alan had been and still was. He kept his word to help him find Michael.

By the fifth day, water was getting very low and when the Twin Peaks Road sign came into view it was a welcome sight, plus seeing the sign *Sunset Ridge*.

Within three hours, several buildings with a river flowing behind them, came into sight. A rider came out to meet them. He asked, 'Do you need water? I see you don't have a pack horse.'

Jackson said, 'Yes. We're very low. We were beginning to worry. We came from the Murray River.'

They rode up to the homestead and dismounted. A thick-set man walked over to them. 'I didn't expect any visitors, but welcome. I'm Stan Rawley. Please come in. What can I do for you?' Suspect criminal or not he was a very pleasant and relaxed person.

Jackson and Alan introduced themselves. 'We were hoping to see your nephew, Michael. We have some business to discuss with him. We believe he is here?'

Stan nodded. 'Yes, he was here. He left two days ago on the riverboat. One of the crew told him people were looking for him. I guess that you were the ones he meant? He left the next day. What's this all about?'

Jackson replied, 'I'm sorry, but it's confidential. Did he say where he was going to?'

Stan said, 'No. Is this about the assault of that woman in Riverbank?'

Jackson remained silent.

Stan said, 'Let's have a drink. It's nearly sundowner time.' He led them into a large room set up as a bar.

Alan thought, *If you didn't know where you were, you would think you were in a typical country outback pub.* The bar was the centre piece with stools, small round tables and the walls adorned with old saddles, whips, horseshoes and even a branded wool bale. The ceiling had old hats nailed to its beams.

Stan asked, 'What will you have?'

They each replied, 'A beer, thanks.'

The three of them adjourned to a table.

Stan asked, 'What do you do for a living?'

Jackson said, 'I'm a vet and Alan is my assistant. We work where we can find it.'

Stan replied, 'I see you are wearing Light Horsemen riding boots. Did you serve?'

'Yes, we both served. I was with the 4th Light Horse Regiment.' Jackson left the room to get Michael's photograph from his saddle bag.

Stan went to the bar and came back with a photograph of a Boer War horseman. 'That's me in Transvaal at Eland's River in South Africa. It was a major supplies depot. I was with the Australian Imperial Bushman. We had it tough. We were under siege for eleven days. The carnage was terrible; hard to forget. The Boers had over two thousand soldiers. We had only five hundred including us three hundred Australians, and they continued shelling us. I wouldn't want that again.'

He paused. 'I guess as a vet he didn't see any action.'

Alan interjected, 'Jackson was at Gallipoli, France and then Palestine at the Beersheba Charge.'

'But I mean he wouldn't have been where people were wounded.'

Alan continued, 'He was wounded twice in battle.'

Stan replied, 'When we went to battle the vet minded the horses. I guess things have changed since my time. Sorry about my inference. I wasn't wounded, but I heard the pains of some soldiers who were wounded near me. They deserved a medal.'

Alan piped up, 'He was awarded a Military Cross.'

Stan said nothing. He felt embarrassed by what he had inferred.

When Jackson returned, Stan pointed at him. 'I thought I knew your face. You were involved in a scandal some time ago.'

'I've put that behind me. I try to forget it. Let's have another beer,' replied Jackson.

Jackson asked Stan, 'Did Michael say why he had to leave?'

He answered, 'No, he knew a few riverboat men and he had been talking with them earlier in the morning. He was quite happy here, so I was quite surprised he made such a quick decision to leave.' He paused. 'How long are you staying. I have plenty of rooms and I enjoy company?'

Jackson answered, 'Sorry we won't be staying.' He asked, 'When's the next south-bound riverboat due? We'd like to travel back to the Murray River. We found the land trip very demanding.'

'In two days I have some supplies arriving. The captain should be able to take you and your horses. In the meantime, make yourselves at home. Feel free to wander about. I'll see you at six for dinner.'

Jackson and Alan walked around the buildings. Stan's station was very well managed. The sheds were clean and functional. A place for everything and everything in its place. The pens and holding paddock fences were well maintained. The stockmen's bunk house was basic. A stockman told them the floor was swept every day and hosed once a week. One half of the bunk house was for sleeping, the other half was used as an amenities area.

Several make-shift showers were outside. He needed to look after his men as it could be difficult to keep good men, when they were so far from a town and in particular, no women.

Dinner was excellent. Josie appeared more than a housekeeper for Stan. They were very attentive to each other. An early night was had by all.

At breakfast, Stan asked Jackson if he would mind having a look at his six milking cows. They supplied the station milk, butter, cream and cheese. He thought they were listless, not their normal selves.

Jackson inspected their eyes, mouth, skin and dung. Their heart rates were a little erratic. Jackson asked, 'Do they have a salt lick.'

'No, not lately. I ran out a while back and I didn't think it was necessary.'

'Well Stan, I suggest you keep supplying them with a salt lick in future. Would you like me to check your stock horses?'

Stan said, 'Follow me.'

The horses were in a yard with a stable attached. It had eight stalls inside. The stalls were immaculate, swept and with fresh hay. Jackson knew that most of the horses would be out being ridden by their stockmen working the station. There were five in the yard and two in stalls. He closely watched the yard horses as they trotted around. Then he gave them each an inspection, paying close attention to their hoofs. The two in the stalls were in foal. Both were carrying well. He checked if the foals were in the normal position. All was good.

Stan watched and said, 'You know your stuff. Thank you. I appreciate your service.'

After inspecting the stock horses, Jackson went for a walk by himself. When he was in the last stall, he noticed some cow hides in the adjacent stall. They were probably meant to be covered over but the corner had lifted, probably by the wind. He remembered what the constable had said about Stan's credibility. He thanked Stan and Josie for their courtesy.

The riverboat, *The River Princess,* arrived early the next morning. They had just completed breakfast. The captain agreed to carry them downstream to the Murray River. He owed Stan a few favours.

As Jackson was about to go aboard, he mentioned to Stan that, in a week or so, he would probably receive a visit from the constable asking after them. He looked straight at Stan and said, 'I thought you should know he will be coming.' Stan smiled knowingly.

The river was flowing slowly. The boat wasn't that much faster either, but it was pleasant sitting on the deck enjoying the sun. Jackson and Alan had both agreed Michael would probably head to Melbourne to his parents. He could easily get a job there, even if he didn't want to work for his father or vice versa.

For the time being they were fishing from a river boat without a care in the world.

When they came to the Murray River, the captain had a letter advising him of a cargo upriver past Riverbank. 'You may as well stay on board,' he said.

They thanked him. 'Yes, it would suit us to go nonstop to Riverbank.'

Jackson had lost track of time. He had not contacted Mary since they had started their journey, over a month ago. That was thoughtless of him.

The River Princess docked at Riverbank at noon. The pair would meet in five days as previously planned, at the pier.

Alan went to Jane's. Her mother was in her favourite place on the veranda, dozing. Alan tied up his horse and went quietly into the house. He knocked on Jane's office door and entered.

She smiled. 'Welcome back. I hope you're staying. We missed you. Mother missed you and your attention.'

Alan said, 'She's asleep in her rocking chair. I'm sorry I didn't keep you informed. I will have to go away again, hopefully only for a week or so.'

Jane replied, 'Yes, of course. Come as you wish but let me know when you are going, for Mother's sake.'

Jackson went to his uncle's business and walked in, calling, 'I'm home.' They were sitting down to lunch. They loved him as a son, and he loved them as his second parents. Happy to see him, they greeted him with a hug from his uncle and a kiss from his aunty who handed him a letter from his parents.

He would read it later She sat him down and placed a serving of stew in front of him. At last! A home cooked meal. During lunch, his uncle gave him an update on the business progress. It had slackened off a little after the war, but they now had figures better than 1916's, their peak year.

After lunch Jackson sat down to read his parent's letter. They were leaving the Queensland property and had purchased a large sheep property near Yass. They were in good health and hoped to see him soon. That was good news. He hadn't seen his parents for several years. Perhaps he and Mary could visit them. He rose early each morning and began to earn his keep – feeding and watering the horses and curry combing the ones he considered most in need. Three horses had to be delivered out of town, an hour there and an hour back. He was now enjoying himself, but evil was still in the back of his mind. At breakfast, he told them he would be away for a several days.

Jackson was waiting in the dark when Alan rode up to the Riverbank pier. He asked Alan, 'Can you be ready to ride tomorrow at sun-up?'

He replied, 'Yes. Where do we meet?'

'At the railway station. We'll travel on the freight train and take our horses with us. I've already arranged it.'

CHAPTER TWENTY-TWO

Pay Back

The train guard greeted Jackson. 'Good morning. Go to the last van and load your horses. You can stay with them. There's tea in the urn.'

Jackson and Alan made themselves comfortable on the rolls of tarpaulin stowed there.

The train ride was relaxing – sun shining, newly shorn sheep in green paddocks and school children waving to the train, even though it was a freight train. It was a good day. After thanking the guard, they disembarked at Melbourne.

They had a leisurely horse ride to Collingwood where they planned to stake out Michael's parents' business and just wait. They were surprised to see so many horse-drawn vehicles. Melbourne had grown. It was now a major city.

The Rawley leather goods business premises was on a corner block in a busy business area with a mixture of commercial and service industries. Most were two story buildings, some with open verandas on the upper floor.

The few with their verandas facing west had awnings for protection from the summer sun. Opposite the front of the Rawley's business was a vacant building with awnings on the veranda. Just the place for a surveillance to be carried out.

They agreed to a week-to-week retainer on the vacant building, telling the agent they were waiting for some finance to be approved by a bank. They purchased some cheap beds and two chairs and a table plus a few blankets.

They started that night to watch the Rawley business, particularly the upstairs windows. One night when Michael's parents were standing at the front of the shop an upstairs light was switched on. Alan was on watch and his heart skipped a beat. He called Jackson. At long last a positive sign. After two more weeks, they decided to spend more time watching the side of the building where there was a side gate. Success! Two nights later, on a moonless night, Alan spotted a furtive figure exit the side gate of the Rawley building and walk down the side street.

Alan followed him to a small pub in a dimly lit back street. He entered the bar and saw a man fitting Michael's description. He was sure it must be him.

Jackson became agitated. He could hardly keep still, and his attitude became very aggressive after he heard Alan's story.

Alan then took him to the pub.

Jackson looked through the window, then stepped back, a strange look on his face. 'It's him.' He turned and they went back to their leased building.

In the morning Jackson put his loaded revolver in his overcoat pocket. That night Jackson watched the side entrance. He did this for a week before Michael reappeared from the side entrance and walked to the pub.

The only light in the street was near the pub's front door. The rest of the street was in darkness. Jackson walked into the darkness and hid in a doorway. It was two hours later when Michael left the pub. He was walking towards Jackson.

When he was within five yards of him. Jackson stepped from the doorway and said, 'Hello, Michael. We meet again.'

Michael froze. He knew that voice. He started to shake from the shock of hearing it and then seeing the man he knew would kill him for his illicit relationship with his fiancée.

Jackson waited for him to say something.

Michael's brain was spinning. What could he say that would save his life? Sorry would not be enough! Finally, he spoke, 'I knew one day you would find me but please don't kill me. I've been running from you since you were released from gaol. I've had no peace of mind. Please to God don't kill me.'

Jackson was standing with his hands behind his back. 'Empty your wallet and throw the money on the ground and then throw your wallet away. God won't help you today.' He now showed his right hand was holding a revolver and he pointed it at Michael's chest.

Michael stepped back as Jackson came towards him. Jackson stumbled on the bluestone gutter. He fell forward, instinctively pulling the trigger of his revolver.

The bullet struck Michael in the groin, and he collapsed in pain, blood seeping through his clothes. His screaming was ignored. The pub owner went and closed the bar door. The few bar patrons ignored the gun shot noise. They were used to violence in this area in the dark hours. It was an hour before a police patrol found him, more dead than alive.

The money strewn around and the wallet on the roadway, suggested a mugging. Jackson had planned well. He had walked back into the shadows and disappeared into the night.

Alan was waiting for him to return. Jackson arrived back and said, 'It's done. We'll leave tomorrow. Let's have a good night's sleep and we can talk about it later.'

The next morning, they went to the leasing agent and apologised for any inconvenience, but they advised they would not be extending the lease. The finance they were expecting had not come through. They handed over the key and left the building.

As they were riding out of Melbourne, Alan asked, 'Well, what happened last night?'

Jackson replied, 'I shot him in the groin. I meant to kill him, but I stumbled and pulled the trigger as I fell. I'm not sure how badly wounded he is, but it's finished; it's over. I feel relieved somehow. Should I feel like that?'

Alan chose his words carefully. 'It's been driving you for a long time and now it's done. I think you're relieved it's over. It's time to move on.'

Jackson nodded, agreeing it was over.

CHAPTER TWENTY-THREE

Michael's Trial

Chief Inspector Gemini first became aware of the name Jackson Carlsone when he was reading the monthly crime statistics. His curiosity was aroused when he saw he had been awarded the Military Cross. Miles had served in Gallipoli and France during the war. A month after Jackson had returned home, he was gaoled. Later that month, he was reading the monthly list of releases from gaol. He remembered the Jackson Carlsone trial of the Military Cross holder and wondered. Why?

When the chief inspector read the transcript of the trial and the court case of the charge of assault and the background to it, he felt an instant empathy for Carlsone. He wondered how many other wives, fiancées or girlfriends had betrayed their husband's, fiancée's or boyfriend's trust!

To be gaoled for giving his best friend a thrashing for cheating with his fiancée seemed grossly unfair, even a morally corrupt decision.

Miles felt he would have done the same thing if he was in a similar situation even though he was a senior police officer! He could possibly understand a girlfriend, but not a wife or a fiancée, when they were away fighting in a war. He made a note in his diary to discuss this crime with the local police when he was next in Riverbank. It was the same town Michael Rawley came from, who was now a person of interest in livestock theft, and attempted rape. His whereabouts was still a mystery.

A detective came to the chief's office with a Melbourne newspaper opened at a page with the story of a man shot in the street. The man said he couldn't remember anything including his name. His photo in the paper was similar to a mug shot of Michael Rawley. 'Well spotted. Let's visit him.'

Michael had been operated on the following morning. The bullet had severed a testicle, torn through a part of his inner thigh muscle and removed a section on one side of his penis. The operation was successful. However, his penis now had a bend in it. It was the favourite topic of the month in the hospital. Some nurses volunteered to change the dressing just to have a look. Michael could still urinate but was uncertain if that was the limit of its use. When would he get the opportunity to see if it would work again?

What would a woman think of his manliness with his bent penis? Would she laugh or just get up and leave him? There was no way he would ever forget Jackson Carlsone for as long as he lived. Jackson had made his mark permanently.

'Are you Michael Rawley?' asked Chief Inspector Gemini.

Michael gave him a blank look. 'I'm sorry, sir. I've lost my memory. I can't remember anything.'

'Well, we know who you are. Your parents lodged a missing person report and they have seen your photo in the newspaper.

'They are waiting outside now. Sir, you are Michael Rawley from Riverbank. I'll let you have some time with your parents and then we'll come back.'

Michael didn't answer; he just hung his head.

When his upset parents came in, he could see his mother had been crying and his father looked worried. They both knew he was in trouble with the police but not to what extent. Neither did he, yet!

When his parents left, the policeman returned. He was initially asked about the bullet injury. Michael had made up his mind; he would not mention Jackson. He had the feeling that Jackson would think justice had now been done. Why? Because he fired only one shot at him. He could have fired the remainder of the revolver's bullets into him. But he didn't. He told the police it was a mugging, and he didn't recognise the gunman.

The detective then asked, 'Do you know a Jane Morris of Riverbank?'

He nodded. 'Yes, I do.'

The detective asked, 'Are aware that a warrant has been issued for your arrest concerning an incident at her property on this date?'

'Yes,' Michael answered.

The detective continued, 'I am placing you under arrest.' After reading him his rights, he was advised, 'A constable will be stationed outside your door until the doctor has given you a medical clearance to leave the hospital. Any questions, sir?'

Twice Wounded

Michael shook his head. 'No.'

Michael left hospital three weeks later and was formally charged and then bailed into the care of his parents with strict home detention rules. He was not to leave the business premises for any reason or he would be charged and remanded into custody. The trial date was set for three weeks at the Riverbank Courthouse.

Jackson and Alan sat under a large gumtree enjoying a beer, watching the river waters flowing by.

Alan had noticed a dramatic change come over Jackson since the shooting. He was more relaxed and was now enjoying life.

He had told Alan about the shooting and that was the end of it.

Justice had been done! The newspaper story was of a mugging that went wrong. The wallet and money on the ground tended to support that story,

The crime became a statistic. Jackson was a little concerned about what Michael might say when he went into the witness box over Jane's assault.

Jackson decided to remain low for a while. He knew of a sanctuary at Bundaloo on the Goulburn River. He remembered a boathouse at Kelly's Landing. It was liveable the last time he saw it. Old Kelly had been a friend of his uncle and had vanished a few years ago and it was feared he had drowned. Jackson had an idea his uncle now owned it. He hadn't asked.

Alan was happy to stay with him. He had no plans of his own yet, although he would probably go back and work for Jane.

The ride to Kelly's Landing was through thick timberland. The track was difficult to find but find it they did.

The track opened out into a large clearing overgrown with weeds. The boathouse was still intact. After hobbling the horses, they went to the front door. A good push and it creaked, then opened fully. Inside was evidence of possums and birds. But generally, it was sound and habitable and most importantly the roof seemed solid and was not leaking. It contained two beds, a table with two chairs and two cupboards with an assortment of cutlery. The beds had old straw mattresses and some rugs.

Alan gave it the thumbs up as well and took the rugs down to the river to give them a basic wash. They soon dried in the sun. A few hours of toil soon had the evidence of possums and birds gone. The boathouse was now habitable.

They found fishing lines and some colourful trout flies made by Kelly. Fishing would help pass the time.

Jackson had done a few scenery paintings in the past. Perhaps he could start doing some more again? During Alan's next trip to town for supplies, he obtained some canvases and paints at the local arts centre.

Jackson decided to visit Mary. He rode during the evening, arriving at her farm around midnight. The barking of the farm dogs woke the entire household.

Mary's father was soon on the veranda with a shotgun. He was taking no chances.

Jackson identified himself, calling out his name loudly.

Mary joined her father. 'You gave us a scare. You weren't expected but come on in.'

Jackson dismounted and followed them into the lounge room.

Her father said, 'Goodnight' and left the room.

Jackson kissed Mary. 'I have to tell you what I've been up to. You know about Michael Rawley?' She nodded. 'Well, I've been chasing him all along the Murray River. I was going to kill him for betraying my trust. I eventually found him in Melbourne and shot him, but he survived. I'm staying out of sight until after his court trial over this rape charge. He hasn't said anything to the police yet, but he may during his trial.'

He looked at Mary. 'I hope I haven't shocked you.'

Mary said, 'No, I had an idea that's what you were up to. I can understand your obsession, but I hope this vendetta will stop now, otherwise our friendship won't last.'

Jackson was surprised by her answer. He nodded. 'Yes, you're right and the vendetta is over, as far as I'm concerned. I know he won't come after me.'

He could see their friendship was still intact. He now decided he needed her in his life forever. He moved closer to her and took her hands in his. Looking into her eyes he asked, 'Will you marry me?'

Mary, with a delighted smile, nodded. 'Yes, I wondered if you would ever commit yourself.' They kissed and sat quietly for a while.

Jackson said, 'I'm living near Bundaloo on Kelly's Landing boathouse until after the trial. We could get married then. What do you think?'

Mary replied, 'I see no sense in long engagements. When the trial is finished, we can set a date. Don't forget the banns take three weeks. We could be married within a month.'

Jackson smiled. 'I always knew you were a good organiser.'

* * *

The local newspapers were full of comment regarding Michael's rape trial. As the trial date came closer, Alan asked Jackson, 'Are you going to the trial? I can go and listen. Hopefully he won't say anything about the shooting.'

Jackson said, 'No, I might stir the possum and I don't want that. It would be good if you could go.'

Alan had an ulterior motive; he wanted to see Jane and offer her some support. As he knew the story of her prior involvement with Jackson, he sensed she would need friends. She saw him as he rode up the lane and waved to him. She took the reins from him and tied them to the hitching rail.

'You're a pleasant surprise. I suppose you know of my situation?'

He nodded. 'If I can help in any way ...'

'I would appreciate it if you were in the court. I don't have too many friends nowadays.'

The day of the hearing was a day to be remembered. Alan drove Jane into town and escorted her to the court, where she sat with the prosecutor. Michael had been transported by rail and taken immediately to the Riverbank Police Station cell. During the previous day, the legal persons had discussed the case and the charge had been downgraded to aggravated assault, as the act of rape had not occurred. This, together with their previous long relationship, could make it difficult to prove. The case was to be heard by a district magistrate, Edmund Hurley.

'All please rise,' ordered the clerk.

The court was full, as expected. The magistrate bowed and assumed his chair.

'Be seated,' ordered the clerk. Plenty of noisy feet and chairs, then silence. Michael was led in and seated.

The prosecutor read the charge. 'How do you plea?'

Michael was now standing up. He looked at the magistrate and answered clearly. 'Guilty, your honour.'

The magistrate asked Michael's lawyer, 'Are there any extenuating circumstances?'

'Your honour, the defendant does not wish to cause Jane Morris any further anguish. He apologises for his actions and is most remorseful and, yes, he does understand the ramifications of not pleading extenuating circumstances.'

The magistrate said, 'The court will adjourn until two p.m.' He nodded to the clerk, who ordered 'All rise.' Again, there was noisy scraping of chair legs on the wooden floor as the audience left the courthouse.

The audience stood outside the courthouse. Most thought Michael's attitude was very decent and considerate of him. They all wondered how the magistrate might view Michael's attitude and comments.

Jane and Alan drove to a tea house. She was calm and relieved she would not have to enter the witness box. She sat quietly, thinking it would be good to discuss her previous relationship with Michael with Alan, but no, she couldn't. What would he think of her then? She had grown fond of him. She was comfortable when he was around.

The courthouse was nearly full when they arrived back.

The clerk repeated, 'All rise.'

The magistrate opened his speech with a grim look. 'Mr Rawley, I find it difficult to condone any violence, particularly against women. However, you appear to be genuinely remorseful and considerate of the witness. Not wishing to put her through the ordeal of being cross-examined and having her recall the fateful events of that night. Also, not offering any excuses stands you in good stead. You have pleaded guilty to assault. After reviewing the facts and from my observations, I sentence you to three years' gaol at his Majesty's pleasure.'

'All rise,' ordered the clerk.

The trial was short – over in a few hours. Michael had said nothing about Jackson. Local reaction was mixed. Some considered Jane may have brought this on herself. Others did not condone abuse of women, regardless of the reason.

Alan drove Jane back to the farm and she invited him to stay for dinner. Her mother joined them for a hearty meal. Their cook was from France and had worked in upper class hotels. They sat by a large open fire, talking about farming mainly, about where they grew up, schooldays, friends etc. Nothing personal was mentioned by either of them. Without mentioning Jackson's name, Alan talked about his recent travels on the Murray and his visit to Melbourne. He said they were family and business trips.

Alan was offered a spare room to spend the night, which he accepted gratefully. He didn't fancy riding back to the boathouse late at night. He had enjoyed the day, but it had been long. He had a good night's sleep.

The next morning, Alan told Jane he would be away for another week or so and would be back then for as long as she needed him at the farm. She gave him a friendly kiss and waved to him as he rode back down the lane.

Jackson was pleased that Michael had said nothing regarding the mugging in Collingwood. They had been at the Landing for a month and they both wanted to move on.

Michael did not enjoy prison. He kept aloof and did not try to find a friend.

His cell mate was called "Whiskers", a little old wizened up person, who was notorious for selling gossip. Michael made the mistake of trusting him.

He was teased in the showers by other inmates over his bent penis. He had acquired the nickname of 'Bendy Dick' and it irked him. This night he came back from the showers in a vile mood.

Whiskers asked him, 'What's wrong?'

He answered, 'I wished he had shot me in the head. I hate him for what he did.'

'Hate him? You know him?'

Michael didn't answer. He had said too much already.

Whiskers left a message for one of his police contacts. Two days later Whiskers was taken to the administration building. He was taken to an interview room where he met one of Chief Inspector Gemini's detectives. He told him he was sharing a cell with Michael Rawley, who was shot during a mugging. He had told police he didn't know who it was, but he had told him that he hated him.

When the detective briefed the chief inspector, he wondered if Carlsone was involved. He decided to meet with him. He had planned to go to Riverbank anyhow because of several reported livestock thefts in the district.

Chief Inspector Gemini laid out the reports and information he had on both Carlsone and Rawley on a large table.

His team had several other cases, but Carlsone not only interested him, he intrigued him. What was the complete story behind the brutal bashing of Rawley? His injuries were extensive. It was not an ordinary street fight. This was a vicious almost psychotic occurrence. Rawley must have known he was living dangerously. He must have realised this was a Frontline soldier coming home after over three years of war. He had earned a Military Cross for bravery in action. He had killed people in the line of duty. Rawley was a first-class fool. He must have known there would be a day of retribution!

Regarding the shooting of Rawley, could Carlsone have done this as payback? If so, when was it going to end? The only way he was going to get answers was by interviewing him.

When he reached Riverbank, he and his detective sergeant went to the police station. Over tea and biscuits, the local sergeant gave them a briefing of Carlsone, Rawley and the femme fatale, Jane Woods. 'Each are from good country stock. They went to school together. The incident when Carlsone belted Rawley could possibly be justified but I think he would have killed him except he was stopped. Several years ago, two shearers insulted his girlfriend and I saw him thrash one of them. He has a violent disposition. He frightens me.'

The chief asked, 'Would he be capable of killing a person in cold blood?'

'In his particular state of mind, yes! Don't forget his wartime experiences.' He continued, 'If you want to find him, I believe he's at a place called Kelly's Landing near Bundaloo.'

The chief stood up. 'We'll go there tomorrow. I'd like one of your constables to show us the way. Thank you.'

The detective asked, 'Is this a look and see or a formal interview?'

'We'll play it by ear and see how he reacts.'

The ride took longer than he expected. They arrived at noon as Jackson was just starting to fry some trout. The chief and his fellow police officers introduced themselves.

Jackson took the initiative. 'To what do I owe this visit by the police? If it is going to be long chat, I'll cook some more fish.'

'It won't take long, but your trout lunch invitation sounds tempting.'

He was watching Jackson's reaction to his introduction. There was none. He reacted as an ordinary, friendly person, without a care in the world.

The chief continued. 'I believe you had a falling out with a Michael Rawley. Have you seen him lately?'

'No,' he answered, as he turned over the trout. 'They're nearly cooked.'

The police nodded in agreement.

The detective said, 'I didn't realise I was so hungry!'

'Take a seat. I'll serve,' Jackson invited. Outwards he appeared calm but inside he was worried. Had Michael said something? Over lunch they chatted about living in the bush and fishing and hunting, and he proudly showed them his latest landscape paintings.

The chief was impressed by the realism in the paintings.

After lunch, the chief thanked him for his hospitality and rode back to Riverbank. The debrief had revealed nothing out of the ordinary. They each commented on Jackson's cool, confident demeanour and his limp. The chief and the detective then concentrated on following up the livestock thefts.

When the police left, Jackson sat down and wondered, what the odds were that they would find some evidence of his involvement in Michael's shooting. He was scheduled to be married in ten days. He had made plans to vanish if Michael ever decided to talk. No one in Riverbank knew his parents had moved to Yass in New South Wales. Neither Mary nor his uncle and aunt.

When Mary told her mother and father she would be leaving the district after she was married, her father said, 'You have just helped us to make a big decision. We're looking at retiring to the Victorian coast. Age is catching up to us and if you don't want the farm, we'll sell it.'

Jackson had a nervous ten days' wait. He was still worried about Michael. The wedding couldn't come quick enough. It was a quiet wedding with only about thirty guests, although half the town went to the church service. He would have liked Alan to be his best man, but he had met Jane with an ulterior motive.

Jackson was unaware Alan and Jane's relationship had changed and their friendship was blossoming. She must never find out that he was a friend of Jackson's.

The wedding went as planned and the newlyweds retired to Mary's farm. The next day they started a train trip to Yass.

Jackson's uncle and aunt missed the wedding. They had gone on a sea trip to Brisbane and were now off into the cattle country to look at purchasing a property. Mary had told her parents that she and Jackson would be going away for a while. Her parents had a date to auction their property and asked Mary and Jackson to be back for that day. Her mother had heirlooms she wanted Mary to have. After tearful farewells, they boarded a train to connect with another train to Yass.

They travelled through rolling farmlands as far as the eye could see – green paddocks with cattle and sheep grazing peacefully. Jackson mused – *This was what we fought for in France.* He remembered the desolation of the French fields – the bomb craters and dead trees and the battle grounds. Would those lands ever fully recover?

A voice interrupted his thoughts. It was Mary. 'Would you like a cup of tea and a scone?'

'Sounds good. Yes, please,' he answered.

Jackson knew his parents had a sheep station named *Woodlea* after his late grandfather's property, but he had no idea where it was. They had planned to stay at a hotel and look around the town for a day or so and ask at the shire office, local police station and post office.

Mary was shopping for some presents for Jackson's parents, when she saw a wagon with a *Woodlea* painted sign. She hailed the driver and asked him a few questions to establish if the property was owned by the Carlsone's.

'Yes, I work for them,' he answered. He was in town for their monthly supplies. When she told him who she was, he said, 'I'll be here until sun-up tomorrow. You can have a ride there with me, if you like.'

Mary couldn't wait to tell Jackson the good news.

The next day they met Mathew, the young stockman, and headed out west from Yass. They travelled all day, stopping only to water the horses. That night they had a meal of fruit, bread and tea. They slept in the wagon on the supply bags. Heading off early next morning, they reached *Woodlea Station* just after noon. There were three people standing on the homestead porch.

Even after all the years they had been apart, he could recognise his mother and father. His mother was the first to wave to him and then his father waved. They were expecting Jackson and Mary but did not know when!

The wagon pulled up alongside his parents. Hugs and kisses were the order of the day plus a few happy tears. The couple were soon sitting at the dining table talking and eating. Questions and answers continued all afternoon.

Mary was comfortable with her in-laws and was soon laughing and smiling with them.

She felt at home in their environment. She and Jackson would be happy there.

Jackson was surprised at the size of his parents' property. The homestead had eight large rooms, excluding the kitchen. There were three barns – one was for shearing, another for wagons and gigs, and the third was a stable, workshop and tack room. There was a separate building for the various workmen which had combined living, dining and sleeping quarters.

The property was three thousand acres and carried two thousand sheep plus an orchard and a vegetable garden. A creek flowed alongside the homestead to complete the picture. Jackson's parents obviously had done well for themselves in Queensland.

They only stayed for two weeks as it was time to return to Riverbank for the sale of Mary's parents' property.

Both Jackson and Mary were pensive about returning. They kept a low profile, arriving half an hour before the auction. They sat with Mary's parents as the auctioneer called the bids. The property sold for just over the reserve.

Mary's mother had packed their heirlooms and asked her to take whatever else she wanted. She also said the same to Jackson.

Mary's father had two guns – a Winchester rifle and an antique shotgun. He gave these to Jackson. 'I won't be using these at the beach.'

They stayed at the property until the removalist had emptied the farmhouse. The farm equipment and livestock had been purchased by stock dealers several days earlier. A visit to the bank and their solicitor marked the end of their association with Riverbank.

The four of them hired a wagon to take them and their chattels to the train station. Hugs and kisses and promises to write. Her parents headed south into retirement on the beach.

Mary was heading back to Yass without Jackson. He was staying an extra day or two to discuss his uncle's business and to do something he didn't want Mary to know about.

CHAPTER TWENTY-FOUR

A New Life

It had poured with heavy rain all night. Jackson chatted with his uncle's manager for a while and then got up. 'I'll go down and see if Kelly's Landing boathouse is all right.'

The foreman said, 'Be careful if the river is up.'

Jackson nodded. 'Yes, I will. I may be away for a while.' He wore an oilskin coat as he headed out. Without telling the manager, he took an extra saddled horse.

When he reached the landing the river was high, and he could see it was definitely going to get much higher.

He had thought through what he intended to do before the rain came, but this helped his plan. He was going to vanish!

First, he started to remove the wall planks with a jemmy. He started on the back wall first, then the planks on a side wall. The boathouse was starting to sway a little. When the planks on the other side wall were almost all removed, the river side front wall began to topple into the river crashing into the pier. Within a minute, the boathouse, with some floor supports and most of the smashed pier, were floating down the river. Only some of the boathouse floor and two pier pylons remained.

The water had risen to floor level as Jackson headed to the Murray River, leaving one saddled horse at Kelly's Landing.

He crossed the river at a bridge further upstream from Riverbank and headed north to a railway station on the Yass line where he was not known. It took him three days riding. Together, with his horse, he boarded the next freight train bound for Yass. He left the train one station before Yass and then headed cross country to his parents' station.

Mary was anxiously waiting for him. He'd said, 'I'll only be away for a few days.' She saw him riding up to the homestead and waved a finger at him as if he had been a naughty boy. Inwardly she was glad to see him and kissed him.

He apologised to her. 'I won't be away again. I promise.' That night he told her what he had done.

She could understand why he had done the vanishing act but wondered if it was too extreme.

He decided to call himself John Carl. It was the name of a fellow Light Horseman who lived up in the Kimberly's in Western Australia.

Chief Inspector Gemini was going over the Rawley shooting incident. The police had interviewed all the residents in the area of the shooting. He noticed the *Vacant For lease* sign on the building on the corner and asked, 'Did anyone check if the building had tenants?

Just because it's not trading, doesn't mean it was vacant.'

The detective went looking for the person handling the lease. He was found in the next block of shops.

When asked he said, 'Yes, we had two male tenants for two weeks, pending finance being available for a lease but they didn't stay. They suddenly returned the keys and left. The two of them were living there. They left beds.'

'Can you give me a description and any other distinguishing features of these tenants?' asked the detective. He wrote the descriptions for him and the fact that one of them had a slight limp. 'What date did they leave?'

When the chief was briefed, he asked the detective, 'Did you realise the date they left was the day after the shooting?'

The detective nodded. 'Yes. And together with their description and the limp, we need to formally interview Carlsone.'

The chief agreed. 'We leave tomorrow for Riverbank.'

The chief asked the Riverbank sergeant if he had seen Carlsone around.

He answered, 'No, not since the day he was married. I suggest you ask after him at his uncle's business.' He pointed out where the business was located. When the chief and the detective arrived, the manager met them.

When asked, he answered, 'I saw him three days ago, when he said he was going to Kelly's Landing to check on the boathouse. It was pouring rain and as you can see the river is still high. He said he would be away for a few days, and I haven't seen him since.'

The ride to Kelly's Landing was a slow and uncomfortable ride. The ground in the heavily treed area had retained the rainwater and made the ground very slippery.

When they got closer to the boathouse the detective commented, 'Are we going in the right direction. I can't see the building.' He was correct, there was no boathouse.

There was a saddled horse grazing and some planks that had been the boathouse floor and two pier pylons; nothing else remained.

The chief looked at the detective and remarked, 'Well, what do we do now? Has he drowned, or has he survived and is injured down-river somewhere?' They decided to head back to town with the horse and hand the search over to the local police.

When they took the horse back to the manager, he confirmed that it was one of his horses and it was a company saddle. He had not realised he had a horse missing until the chief and the detective had left to return to Melbourne. He chose to ignore the missing horse. One out of fifty horses.

Before closing the file on the Rawley shooting, they decided to interview Michael Rawley. When Michael was told that he was to be interviewed by a chief inspector, he wondered just how much he knew about him, Jane and the shooting. Reluctantly he agreed to meet the police.

There were four people in the interview room – two policemen, a warden and Michael. The interview started casually; the chief and his detective were old hands at these interrogations.

After introductions, the chief said, 'We still have an open file on your shooting, Michael, and I want to close it. To do that, I need your help.'

Michael did not respond.

The chief continued. 'We have reason to believe that Jackson Carlsone was your assailant. Would you agree it could be him?'

Michael looked directly at Chief Inspector Gemini and answered, 'No, it wasn't him. I've known him all my life. You're wrong. It wasn't him,' he said as he thumped the desk.

The chief looked at the detective, who asked, 'Did you know he rented the empty building opposite your parents' business for a fortnight and vacated it the day after your shooting?'

Michael stood up. 'I am not answering anymore questions. I want to go back to my cell.'

The chief nodded to the warden. That was the end of the interview. The police left the gaol.

Back at his office, the chief asked his detective his opinion.

He said, shaking his head, 'Well, we won't get far with the victim, who is the only witness and he's saying it wasn't Carlsone.'

The chief nodded. 'I agree. Particularly as Carlsone may be dead. Let's try one more thing and contact Carlsone's parents.'

'I believe they manage a cattle station in Queensland. I'll ring the Brisbane Police and ask them for their help.'

It was a week before the Brisbane Police responded and advised, 'Carlsone's parents have left their employer and, when last heard, they were seeking to buy a property of their own. They used to have a lawyer in

Melbourne who acted on their behalf but we have no information on them – name or address.'

The inspector would have consulted his aunt and uncle, but they were still away, and their manager only had the ship's name they sailed on.

They had left the ship two weeks ago at Brisbane and hired a buggy with two horses and were heading towards Ipswich. That's all he knew.

Jackson's parents' names were still on the Queensland electoral role, but as they had not left a forwarding address they could be anywhere in Queensland or, indeed, Australia.

That was the last task relating to the Rawley case. The file was closed, marked unsolved and then archived.

A week later he received a call from the Riverbank Police informing the chief that it was considered Carlsone had drowned as his body had not been found. Chief Gemini wondered. He had a feeling there was more to this saga than met the eye. However, he let it be.

When Michael was released, he joined his parents' business. He kept to himself, having the weekly drink at the nearby pub. He had a small circle of friends, mainly in the saddlery business. He had the opportunity to have relationships, but his injury kept him very reserved. He was never to marry.

Jane and Alan had become very close; they went everywhere together. The townspeople had mellowed over the years, and she was now acknowledged with a friendly wave or a simple "Hello". Jane and Alan had been together for almost two years, and she wondered why he hadn't asked her to marry him.

One night she asked him, 'Where do you see our relationship going? We have known each other for quite some time.' She faced him, expecting an answer.

Alan looked at her before answering. 'I have been wondering how to talk to you about marriage. I have something to tell you and I hope it doesn't alter your feelings for me.' He paused. 'I'm married. I have a wife. I haven't seen her for over ten years. I don't even know where she is. She left me for another man.' Alan stopped, waiting for Jane to react.

She stood up and walked around the room. She then sat next to Alan. 'I want you to stay with me even if you are married. I lost my first love because of a stupid error of judgement. I don't intend to lose you.'

She leaned forward and kissed him. 'We are virtually married now, except in name. I'll see my solicitor and see if he can trace her and obtain a divorce.'

Alan sat quietly, trying to absorb what had been said. He held her in his arms. 'What a magnificent woman you are.' Alan had finally found his niche and had left his previous life behind.

Jackson had also left his previous life behind. Even though Jackson and Alan had become good friends, they would never meet again,

Mary was expecting her first child. She was sitting on the veranda with Jackson looking into the sunset over the sheep-holding pens. 'I've been thinking about where we were twenty years ago and what's happened during the in-between years. You and I have obtained career qualifications, been to war, seen some of the world, found each other and we live our life on a magnificent property in a beautiful part of Australia, without a care in the world.'

Jackson recalled their school days. Those happy and carefree times when life had few responsibilities and friendships were expected to last forever. As children become teenagers and then adults, events can occur, which change one's direction in life. Jackson felt sad. Life could be cruel. Some friends were now no longer friends.

He thought of Jane, Michael and Mary farewelling him when he was going to war. Michael's betrayal of his trust no longer haunted him. Rightly or wrongly, he felt vindicated for shooting him because of his betrayal. Fortunately, he was now at peace with himself. His violent streak seemed to have mellowed.

He had been twice wounded. First physically, due to bomb shrapnel during the frenzy of war, leaving him with a slight limp. Second, emotionally, at home, by the gross betrayal of trust by his so called – two best friends.

His violent reaction physically marked two people for life. Jane her beauty and Michael his masculinity. Emotionally the three were survivors.

HAD HE BEEN RIGHT OR WRONG?
WHAT WOULD YOU HAVE DONE?

EPILOGUE

Chief Inspector Miles Gemini retired ten years after the Jackson incident. Both he and his wife went to live in Canberra with their daughter. One particular ANZAC Day he visited a local art exhibition. One exhibit drew his attention. It was a painting of Kelly's Landing. It immediately brought back memories of long ago. It was signed "J. Carl". Peering closer he saw a small Military Cross painted after the initials. Dated – "1924". Next to this painting were three more with the same signature "J. Carl" and the small Military Cross but with different years. The last one was dated that year – "1936". He realised Jackson had survived.

He asked the manager of the exhibition if the artist was a local man.

The manager told him the artist was a man named John Carl. 'He arrived in Canberra yesterday, accompanied by his wife, Mary, wanting to sell the four paintings. I purchased them. He said he and his wife, a former army nurse, were off to Western Australia to start a new life after today's ANZAC Parade.'

'When did you see him last?'

The manager walked to the window and pointed to the rider leading the Light Horse Troop. 'That's him.'

John Carl was an imposing figure, sitting tall in the saddle – looking straight ahead. He was in full Light Horseman uniform with his sword and wearing the Military Cross in front of his other awarded medals. It was a clean-shaven Major Jackson Carlsone M.C. Even with his beard removed. It was Jackson Carlsone!

He thanked the manager and went to a nearby hotel and pondered. He decided not to inform the police. Jackson had carried out some horrendous crimes. He wondered how many others would react in the same way if confronted with a similar situation between his fiancée and a so-called best friend.

They had betrayed a trust in the worst possible way, when he was fighting in a war. He had always had a fiery temper, but the shock had definitely affected him mentally for a while. He had made them pay dearly for their deceit with the permanent physical wounds he had inflicted on them.

Besides he would never be convicted without witnesses, and it was over twenty years ago. No jury would be interested in convicting a soldier who held a Military Cross for his actions and the circumstances. Miles walked home. He decided to ignore what he had seen and to leave things as they were. It was now history!

Jackson and Mary had never left *Woodlea Station.* When his parents retired to the New South Wales coastal town of Kiama, they decided to stay at Yass Station. They now had three children and were well-known in local Yass circles. They had no intention of going to Western Australia. Ten years after he "vanished" he contacted his uncle and aunt. They said they had never believed he perished. He was still named in their will! His aunty scolded him for not contacting them earlier. Jackson's uncle and aunt purchased a property in the Queensland hinterland and retired there.

Mary's parents both perished in a bush fire two years after they moved from Riverbank.

Jane and Alan never married. They were unable to find Alan's wife and gave up trying to find her and they just continued living together. They never had children.

DEFINITIONS

ABC	To wash only armpits, buttocks and crotch.
Air Ace	Fighter pilot who has shot down several aircraft.
ANZAC	Australian New Zealand Army Corps
Billets	Buckles to tighten a saddle.
Black Maria	Vehicle to transport criminals.
Blue arm band	Recovering wounded soldier.
Bludger	A slacker or lazy worker.
Bow	Front part of a ship.
Bridge (ship)	Mid upper section where captain controls it.
Brief	Prior instructions/requirements of task.
Brigade	Group of over 1000 soldiers.
Carbine	Short barrelled rifle for mounted soldiers.
Ceylon	Former name of Sri Lanka.
Chute	Restricted enclosure for one horse or cattle.

Davits	Supports for launching a ship's lifeboats.
Debrief	A report on results of a given task.
Dog watch	Navy term for 4-6 pm and 6-8 pm periods.
Eddy	Spiral winds at ground level.
Front	The area where Allies and the Axis battle.
Gaol	British form of Jail (American).
Great bundles	To enjoy something.
Grenade	Cricket ball size – throwing bomb.
Heads	1. Forward toilets on ships.
	2. Land either side of Port Phillip Bay entry.
Hoof	The horny part of horse's leg.
King hit	Cowardly punch from behind.
Knot	Ship's speed – 1 knot = 1852 mtr/ 2025 yds.
Mufti	A military person's civilian clothes.
NAFFI	British – Navy Army Air Force Institute.
N.C.O.	Non-Commissioned Officer.
Over a barrel	Trapped in a situation.
Over the top	Soldier leaving the trenches to go into battle.
Port side	Left side of ship – red colour.
P.T.I.	Physical Training Instructor.
Pugarees	Strips of cloth wound from ankle to knee.
Remittance man	Person paid to stay away from England.
Remount	Horse management barracks.
Regiment	400-600 soldiers.

Sniper	Crack shot rifleman. Loner who shoots enemy.
Squad	4-12 soldiers.
Starboard side	Right side of ship – colour Green.
Stir the possum	Create trouble by interfering in an issue.
Sundowner	An itinerant worker or a drink at sunset.
Tack room	Room for stowing horse riding/driving accessories.
Written off	Not worth recovering or refurbishing.

AUTHOR

John P F Lynch has written several "Factional" novels (fact/fiction), local history books and his autobiography. Most books are in the Australian National Archives, in State/Local Libraries and E-books. The novels are set in the colonial history of 1850 to 1860's with realistic storylines of these heady days. This novel contains episodes of the First World War involving the Australian Light Horse Regiments.

He has travelled extensively during his sixty years career in aviation and visited County Clare in Ireland and Cumbria in England to research his colonial novels.

John is a Member of the Order of Australia, a Knight Hospitaller of the Order of St John of Jerusalem and a Fellow of the Royal Victorian Association of Honorary Justices.

He is an ex-Navy veteran and former President of the Romsey/Lancefield R.S.L. for just on ten years and the former President and Secretary of the Romsey Football Netball Club and is a Life Member of both associations. He is a reserve member of the Macedon Ranges Legacy Group having served as a Chairman of the Group, board member and long serving Sergeant of Arms.

John is a former Vice President of the Craigieburn War Memorial Remembrance Committee. He is currently the Technical Advisor and a Life Member.

He and his wife live in the Craigieburn Retirement Village. He is now retired but continues in community involvement.

OTHER BOOKS

By John P F Lynch

The Convict and the Soldier
The Aborigine and the Drover
The Constable and the Miner
The Shearer and the Magistrate

VICTORIAN LOCAL HISTORY

St Mary's Parish – 1858 to 2006
The Romsey/Lancefield R.S.L. – 1933 to 2008
The Romsey Football/Netball Club – 1878 to 2009
Joseph Hall – Kyneton Pioneer – 1804 to 1872

AUTOBIOGRAPHY

A Lifetime's Journey

www.ingramcontent.com/pod-product-compliance
Lightning Source LLC
Chambersburg PA
CBHW050307010526
44107CB00055B/2139